ALWAYS WEAR PANTS

"You might think this book is about working from home. It's about much more than that—it's about being healthy, happy, professional, and successful in the new world of workplace flexibility. This book is a must-read for every team and organization that is trying to build their principles for how they work together and have success as a team and as individuals. I loved every one of the 99 tips!"

—JOHN ROSSMAN, author of *The Amazon Way: Amazon's 14 Leadership Principles*, managing partner of Rossman Partners

"Kevin is a pioneer in the e-commerce and remote-working arenas. He generously shares his practical and profound wisdom for those learning to work at home. This book will help you manage all the family and technology distractions, as well as the blurred lines between the business and personal world. My accounting firm, bookskeep, has a 100 percent remote team, and our new employees struggle with the exact topics covered in *Always Wear Pants*. This book will be a part of our welcome kit for new employees going forward. Its short chapters and spot-on tips makes this book a must-read for busy veterans in the remote-work field and newbies who aren't sure where to start."

—CYNDI THOMASON, bestselling author of *Profit First for E-commerce Sellers*, CEO of bookskeep

"Kevin Rizer's book is a fantastic manual for modern life at this point. It reminds us of those common sense things that we all thought we should already know but didn't think of. It is also filled with uncommon wisdom that can be extremely helpful for anyone making a living from home. Whether you report to a boss or control your own schedule, I recommend reading *Always Wear Pants*. It'll help you maximize your time, productivity, and headspace around the topic of remote work."

—ANTHONY LEE, internationally recognized e-commerce writer & speaker

ALWAYS WEAR PANTS

AND **99 OTHER TIPS** FOR SURVIVING AND THRIVING WHILE YOU WORK FROM HOME

KEVIN RIZER

 Published by Mandala Tree Press
www.mandalatreepress.com

Paperback ISBN: 9781954801134
Hardcover ISBN: 9781954801127
eBook ISBN: 9781954801141

BUS097000 BUSINESS & ECONOMICS / Workplace Culture
SEL027000 SELF-HELP / Personal Growth / Success
HUM010000 HUMOR / Topic / Business & Professional

Cover Design by Richard Knight
Edited by Justin Greer
Typeset by Kaitlin Barwick
Photos by Austin Gartman

FOR EMMY

The best work-from-home companion
a boy could ever have asked for

2006–2019

CONTENTS

ENVIRONMENT | 33

PRODUCTIVITY | 63

PURPOSE | 117

COMMUNITY & CONNECTION | 141

ACTION | 159

CONCLUSION | 165

ACKNOWLEDGMENTS | 167

ABOUT THE AUTHOR | 169

INTRODUCTION

It was January 2011, and I thought I had won the lottery. A company wanted to hire me, and they were willing to double my salary. The bonus: I could work from home. Immediately, my mind filled with all the possibilities: closing big deals while in my underwear, completing marketing plans as I was lounging on the couch, and participating in conference calls with my favorite show muted in the background.

"THIS WILL BE GREAT!" I THOUGHT. AND IT WAS—UNTIL IT WASN'T ANYMORE.

Working from home is simultaneously one of the biggest blessings and one of the biggest potential pitfalls of our modern society. The promise of more flexibility, comfort and convenience can be interrupted by the constant distractions and competing interests for our attention. In my ten years of working remotely, I've experienced both.

When a pandemic struck the world in 2020, I immediately thought about all of the people working from home for the first time. I saw their funny posts on social media, and I fielded more than a few calls from friends who, knowing I'd done this for a decade now, wanted some advice and pro-tips.

I hope this book helps you realize that working from home can be the biggest blessing you've ever received. I also hope you can learn from some of my mistakes and missteps. Think of this as your blueprint—your guide. Through experimentation and failure, I've found what works, and I am excited to share it with you. Together, we'll explore the six key areas of creating your dream life while working from home:

1. **MINDSET**
2. **ENVIRONMENT**
3. **PRODUCTIVITY**
4. **PURPOSE**
5. **COMMUNITY & CONNECTION**
6. **ACTION**

Maybe you have been working from home for some time and are beat down and done with it, or perhaps you're new to working remotely and you want to make sure you get started on the right foot. Either way, I am confident you can take these tips and apply them to your situation to get more done, be happier, and make the most of the benefits of working from home.

MINDSET

Mindset is the most important part of this book—because it's also the most important part of life. Ask professional athletes, thought leaders, or business leaders, and they will tell you the same thing. Mindset is everything.

Unless we get into the right mindset, nothing else matters. You can have the best office setup, the latest gadgets, and all of the productivity tips and tricks in the world, and it won't matter. The proper mindset sets the tone for everything else.

In this section, we're going to get our minds right!

ARE YOU READY?
LET'S GO!

1 ALWAYS WEAR PANTS

We've all heard stories—or seen a video or two—where a guy is in the middle of an important virtual presentation with his colleagues and suddenly the doorbell rings or the dog starts peeing on the rug. He says to his audience of coworkers and managers, "Be right back!" and jumps up to tend to business—and he's not wearing pants.

Imagine you're this guy, standing in the hallway in some old boxer shorts your mom gave you. What do you do?

Do you go back into the meeting, and act as nothing happened? Crack a joke? Or should you just crawl under the table in shame and unplug the power to the WiFi router so you can end the meeting and face the music later?

Whatever your answer—don't be that guy (or girl) in the first place.

Always wear pants.

Yes, but what type of pants should I wear, you may be asking? Well, I'll be presenting different opinions and options for the ideal work-from-home attire, but ultimately, the decision is yours. Whether you pull up your fancy suit pants or opt for something more casual, say board shorts or a comfy pair of sweatpants, if you follow none of the other tips in this book, do this one thing. My first tip—always wear pants.

 PRO TIP Keep a change of clothes in your office so that in the event you need to jump on a quick video chat with the boss, you can throw on something presentable in a flash.

 BONUS CONTENT Scan the QR code below and feast your eyes on my favorite pants-wearing home-office failures.

2 PREPARE AS IF YOU'RE GOING TO THE OFFICE

Get dressed, eat breakfast, and take a shower. Do sweatpants count?

One of the oldest tricks that work-from-home pros have been using for years is this: prepare for work as if you were actually leaving home and going to an office.

Let's put it another way:

If you worked in a typical office, you probably wouldn't stumble out of the elevator twenty minutes late, in your underwear. You also probably wouldn't go three days without showering or three months without shaving or tending to your beard. And you definitely wouldn't miss stopping by your favorite spot for a coffee and a bagel on the way into work. So why do it when you're working from home?

Keep in mind that even though you aren't physically leaving the house, you are still in effect going out into your community, and your work is going out into the world. Perhaps the best reason to follow this advice is that it affects the way you feel about yourself and the work you are performing.

Ask any number of work-from-home mainstays, and many will tell you this is the thing they've found that has the most impact. Get up at a normal and consistent time, take a shower, and keep a routine as if you were leaving the house. Try it for a few days, and I think you'll agree.

3 DRESS FOR SUCCESS

How you dress says a lot about you. What is your current work-from-home wardrobe saying?

When you work from home, it's easy to fall for the trap of not giving a crap about what you wear. I've been there. Comfy sweatpants, a hoodie, and the most ridiculous fuzzy slippers known to man. Are you guilty? It's okay, most people are. However, just because your wardrobe is comfortable, doesn't make it suited for work. I encourage you to rethink your attire when you head into the home office. Going more casual than you would in a traditional office setting is totally fine. But that might mean jeans instead of slacks and a button-down shirt sans tie—not necessarily throwing all ideas of fashion out the window. What you wear will likely depend largely on what type of work you do, whether anyone sees you doing it, what time of year it is, and perhaps where you live and the climate.

I make an effort each day to think about the work I will be doing. Is it crunching numbers or getting creative? Do I have any video meetings? Am I expecting to catch up with a friend for a virtual happy-hour after work? Then I tailor my wardrobe accordingly. If I have meetings or I am working on proposals, I'll dress business-casual, which for me is a nice pair of jeans and a button-down shirt, a polo-style shirt, or even a nice, solid-color T-shirt. On the other hand, if I am brainstorming my way through the launch plan for a new product or working on more creative tasks, a comfortable pair of sweatpants is totally fine.

The key is to be intentional about the clothes you wear, how they make you feel, and the results that you get while you are working. One of my first bosses used to say, "Dress for the job you want, not the one you have." That advice has served me well in life, and it continues to—even on days when no one but me sees what I am wearing.

4 THE MONDAY-MORNING FEELING

Monday morning tells you all you need to know. What is your current Monday-morning feeling?

When you hear the phrase "Monday-Morning Feeling," what comes to mind? A feeling of dread, discontentment, fear, and doubt? If you're anything like me, you've spent most of your workdays dreading Monday morning. There never seems to be enough time to snooze your alarm clock on Monday mornings. You know you need to roll out of bed and get started, but you'll find anything—any excuse—to delay it just a little bit longer. Whether it's work you're not looking forward to or a meeting with people you really can't stand, Monday mornings have a tendency to carry with them the weight of the world.

Now I want you to think back to a time that this wasn't the case. Do you remember the morning of your first day of a certain grade? Or an important game or event as a kid? What about Christmas or a birthday? How about your first day at a new job you *were* looking forward to? That Monday-morning feeling was quite different, wasn't it?

I use the "Monday-Morning Feeling" as a barometer. When I am looking forward to Monday mornings, maybe even taking a peek at my email on Sunday evening, that is a good thing! When I wake up early, without the help of my alarm clock, and can't wait to hit the ground running because of all of the fun to be had, that is a great indication I'm on the right track. When I start to dread Monday mornings, it's a red flag, something to stop and take notice of and pay attention to. An odd Monday or two here or there is one thing. But if this becomes a recurring thing, it can mean that I am off track and a course correction is needed. How do you feel, right now, about next Monday?

 PRO TIP Some course corrections are minor, like taking better care of yourself, or speaking with a therapist or trusted friend. Others may be more substantial, like realizing it's time for a job or career change or addressing a relationship that is toxic.

5 OBSERVE CASUAL FRIDAY

By integrating fun traditions into your workweek, you keep things interesting. What does casual Friday look like for you?

I've always liked casual Fridays. When I worked in television, most people would dress down a bit on Friday, maybe with a golf shirt and slacks instead of a shirt and tie. The studio crews and production personnel would wear a team shirt or jersey, often sparking rivalry conversations and mild trash-talking. Even the on-air talent would get in on it, and if you looked beneath the desk, you might see shorts and flip-flops, a stark contrast to the buttoned-up look you see on television.

But casual Friday is more than just wearing something, well, more casual.

IT'S ABOUT YOUR MINDSET, YOUR ATTITUDE, THE WAY YOU FEEL.

It's a celebration of all that you've accomplished that week, and a celebration of your individuality. It's also an opportunity to let your hair down, and not take yourself, or anyone else, so seriously. How about a friendly competition with a colleague, or an extra-long lunch break with a friend or spouse also working from home?

I encourage you to embrace casual Friday or another fun tradition to break up the monotony of the workweek. And if your week ends on a Sunday, get creative—sweatpants Sunday has a nice ring to it.

6 DON'T ISOLATE

It is easy to isolate when working from home, but doing so will make you sad and unproductive. Think of a time you experienced isolation or loneliness. How did its impact affect other areas of your life?

This tip is a bit ironic, considering I am writing this in the middle of a global pandemic where we are ten months into a worldwide quarantine. In a way, it's also kind of perfect. Today, it's easier than ever to isolate ourselves in terms of a physical standpoint, but it can also be very demotivating if taken to extremes.

WORKING FROM HOME, EVEN IF NO ONE ELSE LIVES OR WORKS IN YOUR HOME, CAN BE GREAT! IT CAN ALSO BE LONELY. VERY LONELY.

When I first began working from home, I loved the fact that I would sometimes go for days without seeing another human being. But that quickly wore off, to the point where I would sometimes go to the coffee shop and work for a few hours just to see other people and have a real conversation—even if it was with the barista. You will lead a much more productive, positive, and fulfilled life if you make an effort to connect with others, even if it's just virtually.

Here are some ways to break the isolation:

- If you're able to leave your home, set up coffee dates once or twice a week with a fellow work-from-homer, colleague, or friend.
- Host a happy hour at the end of the week.

- Check out an online drawing or painting class—or a poetry reading or jam session if that's more your thing.
- Connect with an old friend on the phone, or, even better, on video calls a few times a month.

Some of the biggest connections I've made have been as a result of mastermind groups. Find some people in your field, ideally outside of your company, and connect with them once a week or twice a month and spend an hour sharing, solving problems together, and collaborating on elevating each other's success.

 Virtual "get stuff done" meetings of one or two hours where colleagues connect and sit in a Zoom room together while they work can be a huge boost to productivity and morale.

7 HAVE A ROUTINE

Routines create structure and improve your mood. What does your routine say about you?

When you work from home, you have the luxury of blending your work routines with your home routines before work, after work, and all throughout the day.

When working from home, there are a plethora of distractions that can derail any tasks and set you back. Your secret weapon? A routine will allow you to make sure that the most important things always get done. After all, wasting an hour on social media shouldn't be routine. But spending time cleaning out your inbox before leaving for the day—that's a good routine.

What do you like to do first in the morning? Check email? Listen to and respond to voice mail? Plan next month's sales meeting? Further, how many times a day do you check email? Do you live there, or only check and respond to messages a few times per day?

Everyone's situation is different, so it's impossible for there to be a one-size-fits-all approach. Taking the time to think about your unique job, personal habits, and what allows you to be the most productive will allow you to establish a routine that makes the most sense to you. Keep at it, because experts say that it takes doing something for two months straight (exactly sixty-six days) for it to become a habit.

 PRO TIP I recommend working on and trying to complete your most important tasks before lunch. That way, no matter what happens in the afternoon, the important things are done. And that feels really good.

8 HAVE A START AND END TIME

Having a consistent start and end time adds structure to your day. Do you have a consistent start and end to your workday? What are your "office hours"?

The other day I was talking with our bookkeeper. She sent me an email, and I replied in five minutes asking her to call me when she was free. As soon as I hit send, she called me. She said, "I knew I had to catch you when it was still fresh in your mind!"

She knows these are my "working hours" and my attention would be focused on work and nothing else, so I would be available now for the call—but maybe not later.

Having a consistent schedule can be a lifesaver. There are two obvious benefits: one, your body will appreciate being on a regular schedule, and two, other people can get an idea of when they can reach you.

ESPECIALLY WHEN WORKING FROM HOME, THERE'S A LOT OF BACK-AND-FORTH COMMUNICATION WITH GAPS. A LOT OF WAITING.

And if you're working in different parts of the day due to time differences, it can be especially difficult. Having an official start and end to your workday can help you and those you work and/or live with know what to expect and plan accordingly.

If you have the flexibility to design your own schedule, take advantage of that! Maybe you work different hours on different days, making room for soccer practice, or meal prep, or whatever life throws at you.

Taking the time to actually create a schedule rather than just "going with the flow" will help you stay organized.

Finally, having a consistent start and end time will make you more productive. When it comes to setting up schedules, designing your optimal workday, eliminating repetitive tasks, and on and on . . . these things are much easier when you have a consistent start and end time. As an added bonus, having an end-of-day ritual will help you fight the temptation to overwork (see chapter 10).

BONUS CONTENT

I've always been fascinated by the work schedules of incredibly successful people. Scan the QR code below to read about the typical daily schedules of a few successful people, including what time they wake up and what time they begin working.

9 WIN THE MORNING

Successful people win the morning. Are you set up to win the morning?

You may think that winning begins when you open up your laptop or respond to the first email. In reality, your success for the day starts much earlier. How much earlier? A CNBC article in 2018 found that successful people like Oprah Winfrey, Tim Cook, and Michelle Obama start their day before 6:00 a.m. Ask successful athletes, CEOs, and artists, and you will notice a trend. Starting early allows you to get a jumpstart on the day. I will confess that I am a night owl by nature, but I have been able to train myself to wake up earlier. The thing I love about starting the day before the sun comes up is how quiet it is. There are no phones buzzing, no emails pinging—there is far less competition for my attention.

EQUALLY AS IMPORTANT AS WHAT TIME YOU WAKE UP IS WHAT YOU DO ONCE YOU ARE AWAKE.

For me, it begins with a cup of coffee and some personal time to read and allow my brain to get up to speed. I have a rule of not checking or responding to email or work messages until I go to my home office, but I will read for pleasure. Next, I like to get active. Sometimes this is an actual workout, but it can also be a brisk walk around the neighborhood with the dog or even a good stretch. I find that engaging my body helps to set my mind up for a good day. Lastly, I make time for mindfulness and meditation before I start my workday. Things like journaling, meditating, or writing thank you cards are a great way to ease into something more productive before you begin your work.

My friend Hal Elrod wrote a bestselling book called *The Miracle Morning*. In the book, Hal details how he designed the perfect morning routine that helped pull him out of the depths of depression following a near-fatal car accident. Hal says there are six key "steps" to your ideal morning routine: silence, affirmations, visualization, exercise, reading, and scribing.

Is it time to make some adjustments to your morning routine? Are you ready to win the morning?

BONUS CONTENT Scan the QR code below to check out Hal Elrod's book, *The Miracle Morning: The Not-So-Obvious Secret Guaranteed to Transform Your Life (Before 8 AM)*.

10 CREATE AN END-OF-DAY RITUAL

Make the end of your workday a habit. What can you do every day to close your office?

One of the things I hear most often from people who are new to working from home is that they actually work too much. For several decades, corporate America pushed back on remote work because they feared people would be lazy and not get enough done. The opposite is actually true.[1]

With no clock-in/clock-out time, no wasted minutes spent standing at the cappuccino machine, no chats with the person in the cubicle next to you, many people actually put in longer hours and get more done when working from home.

THE BEST WAY TO COMBAT THIS TENDENCY TO OVERWORK IS TO HAVE A CLEARLY DEFINED END TIME OF YOUR WORKDAY.

One way to stick to that end time is to have an end-of-day ritual, something you do each day that signals to your brain that your work here is done. This could be anything: filling out your work log, sending in your last update or report to your boss, making a to-do list, straightening up your workspace, putting your supplies or gear away, or taking the do-not-disturb sign off your door.

Personally, my favorite end-of-day ritual is to make a short to-do list for the following day. You can do this on a piece of paper or a glass

---

1. See Nicholas A. Bloom, et al., "Does Working from Home Work? Evidence from a Chinese Experiment," *Stanford Business*, March 2013, https://www.gsb.stanford.edu/faculty-research/working-papers/does-working-home-work-evidence-chinese-experiment.

board, but I prefer to do it on a notepad on my computer. I quickly type out anything I didn't get done that day that I wish to follow up on the next day. I can then add anything important that I want to revisit. This helps me to truly unwind and disconnect from work, because I'm not worried about what I didn't get done. Now I can focus on the time in between work because I know that once I'm ready to start working again, I'll know just where to start.

 Jot down a to-do list for the following day. It will help you to better disconnect and enjoy the time between work.

11 FOCUS ON "THE ONE THING"

By finding your "One Thing," you free yourself from everything.
What is the one thing that you could do that would change everything?

Bills are piling up, emails haven't been checked in a week, and my to-do list is the same as it was last Friday. I feel the pressure of family obligations, work tasks, and social commitments pressing down on me. Instead of feeling motivated, I'm paralyzed, not moving forward on anything.

Ever felt that way?

From time to time, I still feel this way, but I've identified a simple trick to overcome this: I identify the one thing that's holding me back and start there.

I know, you're probably thinking, "But there's way more than one thing!" There always is, yes, and that's fine. But think about the most pressing thing. If you got nothing else done today except for one thing, what would that be?

For me, it's usually a task I've been putting off; an errand I need to run; a conversation I need to have. Once I identify this "one thing," it sets the wheels in motion again, allowing me to move forward with the rest of my tasks.

If you find yourself repeatedly putting something off, consider making that thing the first thing you do in your workday. Making a habit of doing the thing you often avoid will allow you to see it differently, and you may find that it's not as big and scary or painful as you thought.

12 WORK LESS, DO MORE

Wouldn't it be nice if you could work less than you do now but actually get more done? How can you work less and get more done?

The more you work, the more you get done, right? Maybe, but not necessarily. We just talked briefly about the tendency of people working from home to actually put in longer hours than they did when they worked in a traditional office setting. So where did the eight-hour workday come from, anyway? It turns out, it became "a thing" during the industrial revolution. Prior to that, most workers actually put in much longer days—sometimes up to eighteen hours, sweating away in factories and fields. It was the Ford Motor Company who, in 1914, cut their shifts to eight hours. They also doubled starting pay. The result? Productivity doubled.

I argue that for many jobs, we need a new "revolution." Putting in eight or ten hours, just because that's what we've always done, doesn't make sense. According to *Inc. Magazine* and research from the U.S. Bureau of Labor Statistics, the average worker is most productive for around three hours per day. The rest of the time is filled with unnecessary tasks, duplication of effort, wasting time on social media, etc.

BE HONEST. IF YOU WERE DEDICATED AND FOCUSED, HOW LONG WOULD IT TAKE FOR YOU TO GET YOUR WORK DONE EACH DAY?

It's likely a lot less than the hours you think of as "working hours."

I want to challenge you to look at what you do each day and find ways to trim the fat. Are there wasteful and time-consuming processes you can eliminate? Are there tools that can automate repetitive, simple tasks? We will dive deeper into some of these opportunities to save time in a later section of the book, "Productivity." For now, I just want you to rid yourself of the mindset that you work for X hours per day. Be open to the possibility that you could actually get your work done in less time, far less time even. Are you open?

 For two weeks, keep track of your daily tasks and how much time you spend on each with a time tracker. This illuminating exercise will show you where you spend time, and where you can save it.

 Scan the QR code below to access my free time tracker.

13 CREATE FREE TIME

You can shave an hour or two off your workday with a few steps.
What can you do to create free time while working from home?

In chapter 12, I teased you by hinting that it is possible to work less and actually get more done. But how? Below, I've listed out four ways to shave one to two hours off of your workday.

1. **Stop doing other people's work.** Most of us are guilty about just doing what's in front of us. This can sometimes mean it seems easier to just do something, even if that task really belongs with someone else, another department, etc. Are you doing someone else's work?

2. **Plan out your workday.** Many of us wander into our workday without a plan. It's no wonder, then, that at the end of the day, we beat ourselves up because we didn't get enough done. That's not good for anyone, so begin the practice of planning out your workday. Notice I said practice because the habit doesn't happen in one day.

3. **Eliminate gaps in your day.** Once you begin planning out your day, you will likely see that there are huge gaps in your day. An odd twenty-five-minute gap between important meetings, or a two-hour gap between sales calls. Eliminate the gaps, except for breaks you take intentionally throughout the day. Eliminating the gaps is one of the best ways to add time back to your day that otherwise would be underutilized.

4. **Finish the important things first.** One of my favorite time-saving hacks is to begin the day completing the most important tasks. Most people get burned out as the day goes on, and we are less productive at the end of the day. By beginning your day with the most important tasks first, when you are rested and fresh, you will power through them, and the less-important, minimal-brainpower-required tasks will be easier to do when you get to them.

If you're required to clock in for forty hours a week, you can use the free time you have created to get more done. Surely, your boss will notice—and a promotion or raise is likely in your future. More important than whatever hacks you use or come up with to save time is the idea—the mindset—of saving time. Your time is precious. In fact, it's the most precious commodity you have. No amount of money or success can grant you more time. How you spend that time is, therefore, extremely important. And if you don't protect your own time, don't expect anyone else to do so. You will likely find other ways to shave time off of your workday. When you do, I'd love to hear about them. Send me an email: kevin@alwayswearpants.com.

14   STAY HEALTHY

If you aren't taking care of yourself, nothing else matters. How does your health affect your work life?

Why is a chapter about health in the section on mindset? I get it—it might seem a bit out of place. In reality, the health of our body directly impacts our mindset, and vice versa. Additionally, without your health, nothing else matters. How productive you are, how comfortable you are, how much money you make—none of that can overcome the losses that come from poor health.

I make a habit of talking to successful people from different backgrounds and ages; I like to pick their brain about what helped them to find success and overcome challenges. One of the most heartbreaking things you can hear from someone who has made it to the top echelons of success in their field is that they regret not taking better care of themselves. No amount of money or regret can turn back the clock on poor decisions and mistakes made decades ago regarding your health.

WORKING FROM HOME IS A TREMENDOUS OPPORTUNITY TO GAIN MORE CONTROL OVER A LARGE PART OF YOUR LIFE, THE WAY THAT YOU WORK.

It can also present challenges for staying healthy. When you don't need to leave the house to make a living, it is easy to become sedentary and not move enough. It is easy to make poor eating choices and to not pay attention to your mental and emotional health. I am no expert on healthy living, and I don't have all the answers. What I have learned is that paying attention to these three things has made a difference in my life:

1. Move at least an hour a day. Walk the dog, stretch, go for a run, do yoga or hit the gym. My favorite? A five-to-ten-mile leisurely bike ride.
2. Eat well. Don't skimp on food—it's arguably one of the most important things you spend money on. Whatever your diet, make it balanced and enjoyable, and pay attention to how the way you eat makes you feel.
3. Mind your mental health. Asking for help is a sign of strength, not weakness. Depression, anxiety, money stress, and relationship struggles can and do affect many of us. Please know that there is help available, and asking for it when you need it is one of the best things you can do for yourself. Daily practices like journaling and meditation can also help you to maintain a healthy outlook on life.

15 MAKE A GRATITUDE LIST

A gratitude list is an instant boost of positive feelings. Have you ever made a gratitude list? Why not do one now?

MAKING A GRATITUDE LIST IS ONE OF THE FASTEST WAYS TO LOWER STRESS AND IMPROVE YOUR OUTLOOK ON LIFE.

This can be an invaluable tool for managing your mental equilibrium as you work from home. Even in periods of anxiety where life is throwing you challenges left and right, there is always something to be grateful for. No matter where you're at, it could always be worse. If you got through the first chapter of this book and said, "I can do this! I can wear pants." You're at least 50 percent further along than half the people out there, and that's something to be grateful for.

When I take a minute or two to acknowledge where I'm at and the fact that I do have a lot to be grateful for, many of my doubts, fears, and anxieties seem to melt away. Gratitude perpetuates itself. Jotting down a gratitude list has a way of rewiring our brains to focus more on what is possible than what might be standing in the way. We often find we have more blessings in life than we realized.

If this is new to you, start small. But start. Think of a few things for which you are grateful. It could be family or friends, it could be the weather, or a TV show or book that recently entertained you. Jot them down.

For instance, today I'm grateful for my health, my family, earning a living working from home, as well as my favorite mid-day snack: wasabi-flavored almonds—they're amazing!

Your turn. What are you grateful for?

Pin up your gratitude list near your workspace where you can see it every day. Whenever you need a pick-me-up, glance at it. Create a new gratitude list as often as you can to improve your skill of finding new and unique things to be grateful for. I like to put the month and year at the top of my lists and look back at old ones occasionally as a reminder of all the good things that life has thrown my way.

Scan the QR code below for a template to create your very own Gratitude List.

16 SEE OBSTACLES AS OPPORTUNITIES

Obstacles can often be debilitating. What obstacles have you faced, and how can you use them for good?

Do you remember learning to ride a bike? How about tying your shoes? Parallel parking? Okay, that last one is something many of us still struggle with. You may not even remember learning these things. If you could go back and talk to the person responsible for teaching you these important life skills, they would likely tell you about the difficulty and struggle, even the fear that you overcame to learn how to do something that today you do without even thinking about it. In that moment, these simple tasks were monumental and scary—let's call them obstacles.

There are obstacles in your life today too. Perhaps learning a new software program or dealing with a difficult coworker or boss is keeping you up at night. Or maybe crushing debt or a recent job loss has your stress level at an all-time high. These are the obstacles of grown-up you, and they are every bit as scary and potentially debilitating as learning to ride a bike was for younger you. They're also every bit as surmountable. We are hard-wired to overcome obstacles. It's in our nature as humans. So what changed between then and now? Mindset.

When it comes to the way we see obstacles and challenges, mindset determines whether we stress and allow ourselves to be paralyzed by them or dive in and overcome them.

WHEN YOU SEE THE OBSTACLES YOU FACE AS AN OPPORTUNITY TO LEARN AND MOVE FORWARD, YOUR OUTLOOK ON THE THINGS CURRENTLY STANDING IN YOUR WAY BEGINS TO SHIFT.

If you want to see a living example of seeing obstacles as an opportunity, spend a few minutes watching kids playing on a playground. There, you'll see kids solving all kinds of problems and doing much more than they ever thought possible. Watch the timid young boy look up at the tall slide, afraid to climb up the stairs. Then watch as, encouraged by the positive form of peer pressure, he scales up the steps. See the unbridled joy as he slides down, the wonder and amazement in his eyes as he gets to the ground safely and then immediately takes off running for the stairs again.

Better yet, if there is a playground near you, go there now. Slide down the slide. Imagine that big, scary slide as the biggest obstacle in your life right now. It's time to face it. To see it as an opportunity.

 Ryan Holiday has an excellent book, titled *The Obstacle Is the Way*, which delves deeper into the theory outlined above. If this is a subject that interests you, I highly recommend Ryan's book.

17 FOCUS ON TODAY

Yesterday is gone, and tomorrow isn't here yet. How can you minimize distractions and focus on today?

One of my early mentors picked up on a negative tendency I had. He used to tell me, "Kevin, you've got one foot in yesterday, and another in tomorrow. You're pissing all over today."

He was right. I held on to things way too long, replaying conversations I'd had and the way I handled situations. I regretted a lot and wondered whether I should have done things differently. I also worried a lot about the future. That big opportunity coming up, I hoped I wouldn't blow it. How would I increase my pay so that I could get ahead in life? It spilled over into all aspects of my life: finances, relationships, happiness—and my productivity at work too.

BEING PRESENT AND FOCUSING ON TODAY IS A LEARNED ATTITUDE, NOT SOMETHING YOU CAN SIMPLY SPEAK INTO EXISTENCE.

It does start with that first step, though. Thinking through ways in which you often spend time in the past and the future and making a commitment to stay focused on the here and now sets you on the path toward correcting this damaging mental mind trick. Write the following two affirmations somewhere you can see them while you work, and when you find your mind replaying the past, or trespassing on the future, use them as a reminder:

- The past is over. What can I learn from it? What will I do today to pay respects to all the past has taught me and to march forward with the tasks of today? I commit myself today to being in the moment and to taking life as it comes. I have the skills, knowledge, and desire to effect positive change in my life, right now.

- The future is not here yet, and it is never promised. I will not fret over it or stress about it. Today, in this moment, I am focused on what I can do to live my life in an authentic and positive way. Today, I am preparing myself for all of the good in the world, and I am committed to being a part of that good, for myself and for others.

Affirmations can be a powerful tool to shape your outlook on the world. It's not just froo-froo stuff, either. It really makes a difference, not just in how you feel but also in how you live life.

Scan the QR code below for access to other affirmations you can use.

18 GIVE YOURSELF A BREAK

Don't be so hard on yourself. We are all on a journey. What is one way you need to give yourself a break?

Be honest. Who is your worst critic? For most of us, it's ourselves. Isn't that crazy? Not a spouse or a child, not a boss or a difficult coworker. Not even a creditor or the person we cut off in traffic the other day. Ourselves. This is my request to you: **Give yourself a break.** You are human, and you make mistakes. I want you to learn from them and move on. You'll make other mistakes along the way. That's okay as well.

WHEN WE ARE HARD ON OURSELVES, WHEN WE REPLAY NEGATIVE THOUGHTS AND EMOTIONS, SOMETHING DANGEROUS HAPPENS—WE START TO BELIEVE THEM.

That "head trash," as I like to think of it, creeps into other areas of our lives. It's difficult to have a healthy relationship if you are constantly beating yourself up over shortcomings at work. Conversely, if you constantly feel like you're not enough for your partner or kids, it's almost impossible to be your best self at work.

The journey we're on is long and winding, full of many ups and downs. And for that journey, you need to be at your best. Plenty of other people will take shots at you along the way, and unfortunate events will sometimes occur. Guess what? There's a lot of good things in store too. Things will break your way, and life-changing opportunities will come. Be ready to receive them by owning the fact that you are okay, by being the best version of yourself today, and by giving yourself a break when you fall short. You're worth it!

BONUS CONTENT
Scan the QR code below for stories of people who have overcome immense personal failures and have achieved great things, after learning to give themselves a break.

— — —

Following the tips in this section, you will have the proper mindset to accomplish anything you desire working from home. Refer back to these chapters whenever you need a boost, or feel that something is off or amiss. Remember that your mindset is the foundation upon which everything else is built.

Now that we have our minds right, it's time to start building on that foundation.

ENVIRONMENT

With the proper mindset in place, the next stop on our make-over of our work-from-home lifestyle is our environment. Your environment while working is critical to not only your success and productivity but also to your happiness.

Have you ever had a crappy office? I mean one where the desk is wobbly and way too small, the chair kills your back after just an hour, and the office one floor up is a testing lab for home theater systems—hello, distractions!

You may feel that your current home office setup isn't much better. In this section, we will focus on creating a workspace at home that is conducive to the work you do and allows you to do it in style and comfort.

ARE YOU READY?
LET'S GO!

19 CREATE A DEDICATED WORKSPACE

Remote workers need a dedicated space, but few have one. Is your current workspace serving you?

At certain points in my career, I've had to get a bit creative with my workspaces. I've recorded podcasts for hundreds of thousands of listeners from a hotel bathroom. I've conducted pitch meetings with millions on the line from my parent's dining room table. In fact, I started my business on a folding card table with a couple of rickety boxes as a chair. Working from home, or working on the fly, means being adaptable and doing the best with what you've got, and sometimes that means unusual working spaces.

Ideally, you will have a separate room in your home that you can use as an office. Once you designate this area, protect that space. Don't use it for playtime with the kiddos or fireside chats with your significant other. That's your office. You will find that you get more done if you use your office for work and the rest of the house for living. Minimize the distractions by removing unnecessary clutter and non-business-related reading material, and turn off the TV if one is present.

FOR THOSE THAT DO NOT HAVE AN EXTRA ROOM TO SPARE, YOU CAN STILL HAVE A SPACE THAT IS DEDICATED TO WORKING.

In this case, do the best with what you have. Whether it's the kitchen table, a corner of the living room, or a comfy place outside on the patio, make it your own for your work hours. Establish a sturdy writing surface, ensure you have all of the necessary tools you need (computer, chargers, writing pad, and pens) and get to work. Let anyone else living in your home know that during work time, this area is devoted to your work.

In a chaotic mixed environment, nothing gets done, or rather, nothing gets done well. With excess junk in your way or a pile of dirty dishes behind you begging to get washed, you lose the ability to focus solely on your work and invite constant disruptions into your work-flow. You'll see that setting aside a place dedicated to work makes a huge difference in your mental attitude and your overall productivity.

If working from home is the new normal, then I'm giving you permission to use your imagination a bit. Look at that spare bedroom that nobody ever sleeps in, or that forgotten corner of the basement, and say, *Hey, this needs to be my new home office.*

Although it may seem like a comfortable spot, the couch is not the most conducive space to plant yourself and be productive long term. Instead, opt for the kitchen or dining room table.

20 GET A PROPER CHAIR

Don't break your back with a bad chair. Do you need to update your seating arrangement?

Having a proper chair is essential when working from home. But what exactly is a proper chair?

It's up for interpretation, but for me, posture trumps everything on the list when looking for a great desk chair. Find a chair that makes you feel good and that is comfortable to sit in for long periods of time. But not too comfortable. Resist the temptation to claim the couch as your chair or slump down in an oversized recliner. It may sound good now, but your back will hate you for it later.

The best desk chairs are a mix of comfort, style, and function, with style taking a backseat to comfort and functionality. I'm a big fan of being happy and proud of your work environment, but at the end of the day, if you're killing your back sitting in a stylish sexy chair—that's not a great long-term solution.

Also, remember, you're supposed to get up every once in a while and move around. So, it should be comfortable, but not comfortable enough to fall asleep in.

 PRO TIP If your current chair situation is less than ideal, improve it by placing a pillow or cushion under your bum, or place a pillow behind your back to provide more support.

 BONUS CONTENT Scan the QR code below for links to great chairs for any budget.

21 INVEST IN OR CREATE A GREAT DESK

The coffee table won't cut it. What do you use for a desk?

Having a proper desk is as important as having a dedicated workspace in your home. The coffee table? No. The TV tray you've been putting your laptop on? It's got to go. And the kitchen table, while good in a pinch and okay for the short term, is not optimal either.

HAVING A PROPER DESK TO SERVE AS YOUR HOME BASE WHILE WORKING WILL DO WONDERS FOR YOUR MOOD AND THE WAY THAT YOU APPROACH YOUR WORK.

You might find that it gives your productivity a boost too. Fortunately, gone are the days of cumbersome "built-in" home office desks, complete with slide-out trays for the keyboard or clunky filing cabinets. With computers getting slimmer and most filing moving to digital solutions, you can get creative with the style and functionality of what you call your desk.

I know successful work-from-homers who have beautiful, elaborate home offices. I also know multi-millionaire entrepreneurs who live out of a suitcase, and their office is rarely the same from week to week.

My "normal" everyday desk is a cheapy from Ikea—a standing desk. No drawers, just a big, flat surface with plenty of room for my monitors, keyboard, and papers or trinkets. I also have an old antique desk that my grandfather made some sixty years ago. I had it restored recently, and I use it if I'm writing, reading, signing contracts, etc.

Whatever you decide, the two most important things about a desk are these:

1. It is functional for your work purposes.
2. It is at the right height, allowing for proper ergonomics while you work.

Standing desks allow you to sit or stand with ease and to switch back and forth throughout the day. I like standing desks because they allow me to stand for a few minutes, preventing me from getting fatigued, while still working. Don't have budget for a standing desk? Make one by finding something, even a box, that you can put your computer on when you want to stand up for a while.

22 PRACTICE PROPER POSTURE

Posture changes everything. How might your posture be impacting your productivity?

There are experts in the field of body posture, and I am not one of them. Fortunately, you don't need to be an expert to take control over your workspace. (Everyone's got a skeleton, after all.)

If you worked in an office before, chances are they bought actual office furniture that is theoretically decent and adjustable. At home, we make do with what we have. We're more likely to grab a chair from the dining room or put our feet up on the coffee table than we are to run out and buy a thousand-dollar ergonomically adjustable office chair.

Still, it's a good idea to know what's available and what a proper desk setup actually looks like. When you are designing your work-from-home setup, keep posture in mind. Here are some general rules:

1. Ensure that your chair not only looks good but functions well (see chapter 20).
2. Make sure that your desk is at a proper height and angle, so you're not craning your neck, and that your keyboard, mouse or trackpad, and monitor feel good and don't cause strain on your wrists when you use them.
3. If you utilize a standing desk, which I highly recommend, consider a foam mat or other pad to stand on to relieve stress on your feet.

BONUS CONTENT Scan the QR code for a short video from an occupational therapist, instructing you on how to properly set up your working space to make it more ergonomically suitable and help maintain proper posture throughout the day.

23 EAT LUNCH SOMEWHERE ELSE

Leaving your desk to eat lunch provides a quick refresh. Where can you go to "get away" for lunch?

Do you remember the internet meme "sad desk lunch"? Thousands of workers posted images of unappetizing-looking takeout, hastily packed lunches, and prepared foods sitting at their workstations. It was the sad, but true, reality of working in an office.

As a work-from-home person, you have options. You don't have to have a "sad desk lunch" if you don't want to. And while changing your environment might not make your lunch any less sad, at least it'll give you a change of scenery!

Admittedly, I'm guilty of skipping a lot of lunches. I never used to leave my desk, and especially not for something so trivial as lunch. If there was a reason to leave my office, like a lunch meeting, I would gladly attend. But if I was just making a sandwich—nine times outta ten I was going to devour it while I was working. I've just recently broken this habit, and thankfully I no longer eat at my desk.

It's very important to take a lunch break.

FIGHT THE TEMPTATION TO EAT AT YOUR DESK AND "GET MORE DONE."

Regardless of whether you're dining on leftovers or not eating at all because you are intermittent fasting, a midday break to recharge and refresh can do wonders for your work life.

If you're reading this book during a global pandemic, heading out to the local sandwich shop to meet a friend for lunch might not be possible. Even still, go somewhere other than your workspace for a lunch break. This is the perfect opportunity to take advantage of working from home. You can use the time to watch an episode of your favorite TV show or sit outside and soak up some rays if the weather is nice.

Preparing your lunch the night before, or the morning of, your workday gives you something to look forward to and makes it much more likely you'll actually take a lunch break and enjoy it.

Scan the QR code below for a few of my favorite work-from-home recipes. Then share your own with me—email me at kevin@alwayswearpants.com.

24 HANG A DO-NOT-DISTURB SIGN

Hang the sign and know when to use it. What can you do today to set a workplace boundary with your family?

A friend of mine gave me this tip. Personally, I don't have a do-not-disturb sign, because I don't have kids. But if you do have a family, this is invaluable.

There are times when you're going to have important meetings, a video conference with your boss, or a new client you want to impress, and the last thing you need is unwanted interruptions. Striking that work-life balance at first, however, can be a challenge. Creating some visible cue for those sharing a home with you will help them know when you can be interrupted and when it's better for them to wait.

Just as important as setting this boundary, however, is knowing when to use it. If you do decide to hang a sign, use it for specific reasons. Don't just hang it out there all day, every day.

Reserve use of the do-not-disturb sign for only the most critical parts of your day. The few hours where you really need to hammer out that report that's due, or a meeting that would be negatively impacted if the kids ran in or the dog started barking. In other times, welcome the opportunity to have those momentary disruptions and enjoy the little things in life. Your kids or spouse should be able to stop by with cookies or a snack or to show you something they created sometimes.

You don't want to lose out on that flexibility—otherwise, what's the point of working from home? So, know when to use it.

BONUS CONTENT Scan the QR code below to create and print your very own Do-Not-Disturb sign.

25 SEPARATE HOUSEHOLD CHORES FROM WORK

Just because you work from home doesn't mean you should work on your home. How can you keep your work and household tasks separate?

On your ten-step commute to the office in the morning, you notice laundry piled up by the washer. The sink is overflowing with last night's dishes, and you remember the burned-out lightbulb your partner has been asking you to change for two weeks. Working from home gives you the opportunity to mix work and household chores, but just because you can doesn't mean you should.

So much of the good of being able to work from home is eliminated if you allow the two things to blend without boundaries. Just as it's important to have a dedicated space and to expect yourself and others to respect those boundaries, it's also important not to mix your work with household duties. The dishes can wait, and the laundry will get done eventually. When you're at work, work.

One caveat to this is that I like to sometimes use a quick fifteen-minute break from work to accomplish something around the house . . . the key is making this break intentional, and scheduling it. This can be folding laundry or putting the dishes away. This quick mental break refreshes my mind and allows me to get something done around the house too. It's a win-win. If you live with others, it is especially helpful to set the expectation of when you are working, and when you are available to help out around the house. Balance is key here, and striking the right balance will allow you to focus on work when you are working, and not working when you're home.

26 TURN OFF THE TV

It might seem like harmless white noise, but the TV can be a big mistake. What can you do to fill the void of the TV while you work?

What in the hell are you watching? How is it helping you to be more productive, happy, or focused? Is it going to get you the raise or promotion you're hoping for? Odds are, it's not.

I have a confession: As someone who spent more than ten years of my career in the TV news business, it's been all too easy for me to fall into this trap. I tell myself that I am staying up-to-date and connected, or "on top" of things. I tell myself it's just white noise. I tell myself that having a program in the background is no big deal. And then I get less done. I get distracted. I end up on the couch, bingeing the latest season of my favorite show.

There are exceptions, of course, when watching TV in the middle of the day is acceptable: historic events, emergency broadcasts, or if you're the type of business person who needs to watch the stock market, for instance, or a PR person who needs to keep up with current events. But for everyone else—seriously, there is no reason to have the television on (or YouTube!) while you work. Instead, turn it off and get some stuff done. Then, you can relax and watch whatever it is your heart desires, guilt-free, with the knowledge that you crushed it and can now indulge.

BONUS CONTENT Scan the QR code below for a list of my favorite binge-worthy shows. Want to share yours with me? Text me at (972) 850-2141. I may just respond to thank you.

27 USE NOISE-CANCELING HEADPHONES

Audible distractions can kill your work mood. Do you find noises distracting? How have you coped?

I remember the first time I tried a pair of noise-canceling headphones. I was on a five-hour flight with a crying baby behind me when I put them on. The difference was astounding, and these weren't even that great (this was about ten years ago). I've never been able to sleep well on planes, and I managed to get a decent nap in before we landed. I thought, *If it works that well on a plane, imagine how well it will work from home.*

As a work-from-home person, you have the luxury of not dealing with the conversation in the cubicle right next to you or phones ringing, but there will definitely be household noises. There are a number of things that can distract you when working from home. Screaming kids. Barking dogs. The hum of the lawnmower from your neighbor who rarely mows the lawn but for some reason has decided to . . . right when you've got a tight deadline.

If you're doing something that requires a lot of focus, noise-canceling headphones can be a smart thing to invest in. For me, they're a lifesaver. You can play music, listen to a podcast, or soothing sounds, or just use them in all of their raw glory to hear . . . nothing. Yes, they can be pricey, but in my opinion, the value you get in return is worth it.

 BONUS CONTENT Scan the QR code below for a link to several models of noise-canceling headphones I recommend, at several different price points.

28 SET THE MOOD WITH MUSIC

The right music makes all the difference. What five songs are at the top of your WFH playlist?

Now that you have some noise-canceling headphones . . . to music, or not to music? That is the question!

To each their own on this one.

For me, it depends on the situation and what I am working on. I will admit that I was slow to come around to the concept of having music playing while working from home; I always opted for the quiet and solace of having nothing in the background. One day, I decided to play some smooth jazz early in the morning, and it was life changing. Next, I put together a hard rock playlist for just after lunch to reinvigorate my mindset. Now, I'm a convert to the powers of influencing your mood and affecting the way you work with music.

Still, there are times where my need to focus is best quenched by peace and quiet. In that case, just the sweet sound of silence will do.

Maybe you'd like to explore music options but don't know where to start? If you are on a subscription service such as Spotify or Apple Music, you can find ready-made playlists that are appropriate for studying or working. If you don't like music with lyrics, you can find classical playlists, or listen to relaxing sounds, for instance. There's even music with alpha waves layered into it for superior focus.

BONUS CONTENT Scan the QR code below to access the "Always Wear Pants" playlist on Spotify.

29 USE A GOOD MICROPHONE

A good mic is essential to be heard by those that matter.
How can you make sure your voice is always heard?

This tip is for everyone, but especially podcasters and anyone that creates content regularly. Your audience cannot see you, they cannot touch you, and they cannot smell you (hopefully). They rely on their ears, and if you sound like you're talking into a tin can, it'll be a distraction. Regardless of the reason for the meeting, broadcast, or live stream, having your listeners cringe every time you speak isn't great.

These days, you don't have to go super fancy to have decent audio quality for things like Skype calls or Zoom meetings, but generally, the built-in microphone with your computer isn't the best for anything where your audience may be listening to you for long stretches of time. Just like I encouraged you to invest in a decent pair of headphones in chapter 28, I will also recommend investing in a decent microphone.

If you're going for the "guru" podcaster vibe, a boom microphone along with a HEIL or other pro-line microphone will look really good and sound even better. If you're just looking for a cheap, good fix, there are several headset USB microphones that cost around $20-30 and sound pretty darn good.

The point is, you don't live inside a tin box, so why make those forced to listen to you think you do? Up your sound-quality game by getting a decent mic.

BONUS CONTENT Scan the QR code below for a link to several microphones at various price points.

30 LEVEL UP YOUR LIGHTING GAME

Elevate your video meetings with good lighting. How can you improve your lighting setup? Is it time for a new lamp?

It's hard to imagine, but in the early days of my business, I used to spend six to eight hours a day on video calls. As a result of a lot of trial and plenty of error, I learned a variety of hacks and tricks for hosting decent-quality video conferences and making the experience generally less painful.

IF VIDEO CONFERENCES ARE GOING TO BE A PART OF YOUR NEW WORK-FROM-HOME REPERTOIRE, IT'S TIME TO UP YOUR GAME.

No one likes being on a video chat with a colleague who is blurry, has dogs barking in the background, is hard to see, or is trying to drive down the 405 at seventy-five miles an hour. Generally speaking, if you abide by a few good rules of thumb, you'll have compliments rolling in.

1. Use the best camera you have. If you don't have a good one, scan the QR code below for a link to one that's terrific and only around $25. Extra tip: Make sure that your camera is stationary during the call. If you're using your phone or tablet, prop it up on your desk or table.
2. People take video calls while they're driving. It's not always avoidable, so if you have to drive, warn people first, and turn off the camera. No one needs to see you dodging traffic. Make it an audio-only call instead.
3. Avoid being backlit by a window or a bright light like a lamp during a video call. Instead, position yourself so that you are

looking at the window, which is a great source of natural light. You can also increase the brightness of your computer screen to mimic this effect.

4. If you don't have adequate natural light or access to additional lighting in the room, consider purchasing an inexpensive light to use for video calls. Use lighting sources in the room such as lamps to add light. Remember: It's better to have lights in front of you than behind you. An accent light in the background may look nice, but it doesn't help your video quality.

5. Test different backgrounds and setups to see what elicits the best results.

BONUS CONTENT

Scan the QR code below for a video walk-through on upping your video game, as well as links to inexpensive products you can use to improve your setup without breaking the bank.

31 BE MINDFUL OF YOUR BACKGROUND

In video meetings, what is behind you matters. What do people see when they peek over your shoulder?

When Zoom meetings became "a thing" during the early days of the pandemic, I was amused. I had been using Zoom for years, managing a remote team. It seems that with everyone using it, some of the lesser-used features went mainstream, one among them being virtual backgrounds. All of the sudden, there were people sitting on the beach, or high up in the mountains, or with a hastily put-together logo behind them.

Being mindful of your background when you are on video calls is about more than just avoiding the cheesy virtual variety, however. Dirty clothes piled up on the couch behind you, or that book that might be a bit off-color sitting on the bookshelf just over your shoulder—these all send the wrong signals. Pay attention to what is behind you, because rest assured when you're stuck on an hour-long call with the boss, there will be plenty of time for him or her to see exactly what's going on in the background.

A few tips for curating your background:

1. Keep it simple. Less clutter and noise is always best. Allow yourself to be the star of the show.
2. Have something behind you. A plant, or tasteful picture, or a few books on a shelf are better than a blank wall.
3. Turn on your camera a few minutes before a video call to see how you look and what's behind you. The day could be hectic, and you never know what might have crept into your background. It's better to fix it before getting on your call than to be embarrassed and frantically trying to fix it after everyone else joins.

32 GET CREATIVE WITH A WHITEBOARD

When you have big plans or problems, a whiteboard provides the space to work them out. Where can you capture creativity while you work?

All businesses need a whiteboard. But especially businesses that involve visual or creative skill sets, strategic planning, and large-scale thinking.

One of the best investments I've ever made is in a whiteboard for my home office. The one I have now is actually made of glass, and it covers an entire wall in my office. (This is the second glass board I've owned; the first one shattered into a million tiny pieces during shipping.) Although this whiteboard is enormous, I've had smaller ones over the years, some mounted on the wall, some on an easel, some just leaning against the wall. They all worked just fine.

There are dozens of uses for a whiteboard, but here are just a few ideas:

- Write a to-do list.
- Map out complicated projects.
- Reorganize information.
- Use it during a meeting or planning session.

There is just something about having space to quickly put information "down" onto a board, and the flexibility to easily make changes, or erase and start over, that a whiteboard gives you that a pen and paper or using a computer does not.

There are also software tools that allow you to do this, and if space just won't allow for anything else, this can be a good option. I highly suggest a more old-school approach, though—it engages a different part of your brain to write something out on a physical surface.

33 CURATE YOUR WORKSPACE

Be intentional and protective about the items you place in your workspace. What is in your workspace currently? Is it serving you?

I have a confession to make to you: I can be a bit of a packrat! Anyone else? Okay, now that I've gotten that off my chest, I feel better. I'm not a hoarder by any means, and I absolutely hate clutter in the rest of the house, but my home office has a tendency to become a bit of a graveyard for stuff. Product samples, file boxes full of old contracts and statements, and things I think I probably won't ever need again, but you can never be sure, right?

CLUTTER IN THE PHYSICAL SENSE HAS A WAY OF BECOMING CLUTTER IN THE MENTAL SENSE TOO.

Spend your days working among a bunch of junk, and you'll find you are more easily distracted, less focused, and less proud of the work you do. A clean, well-curated workspace, on the other hand, will clear the way for a happy, structured, and enjoyable place to spend your time.

Having a curated workspace is about three things:

1. Eliminate the clutter. If it doesn't belong in your office, get it out. Box it up and put it in the closet, or the garage, or the attic, or a storage unit. If it worries you that you may need it and not be able to find it, create a list on your computer of everything you are storing and where, and label those boxes. If you know you won't need it, then the best option is to

simply get rid of it. If someone else could benefit from it, consider donating it to charity.

2. Everything has a place. Spend some time thinking about the things you need and when you'll need them, and then place them where it makes the most sense. This can include charging cables, reference materials like books and training guides, and gadgets you may use occasionally, but not daily. When everything has a place, it's much easier to tidy up when things start to look a little out of hand.

3. Add meaningful things to your space. The perfect home office is not just about reducing the clutter and giving everything a home. It's also about enjoying the space. This might mean placing a photo of your kids in the perfect spot on your desk, or pinning a note from your partner right by the door so you see it each time you walk in.

Why not spend some time right now looking at your workspace with a fresh set of eyes? Do you have some decluttering to do? What can you add to your space today to make it more *you*?

34 BOOST YOUR MOOD WITH A SUNLIGHT LAMP

Some 70 percent of people are affected by seasonal affective disorder. Do you notice your mood changing in the colder, darker months?

Some places like Southern California and Florida get a lot of sunlight, but other areas, such as Washington State and Oregon, can be very dark and dreary during the winter months. My partner used to live in Finland and had to deal with almost no sunlight a few months out of the year. The way he describes the extremely long nights that stretched into days there was unforgettably grim.

Not all of us live in extreme climates, but seasonal affective disorder is a very real thing. During the winter, when the days are shorter, millions of people, like myself, get depressed. Sunlight is important for lots of reasons. Without it, plants wouldn't grow, and we wouldn't have food to eat. Research also shows a strong correlation between lack of sunlight and rates of depression in the wintertime when people have very little access to vitamin D.

As far as I know, there haven't been any studies done on the effects of working from home, but I'm willing to bet there is also a correlation between spending so many hours inside and lack of sunlight as well. Either way, it's not a bad idea to invest in a decent sunlight lamp (they're also called SAD lamps). Turn it on for your first half-hour of work. Fire that thing up again after your lunch break to get you back in the zone. And especially use it during those dark winter months. I think you'll notice a difference.

BONUS CONTENT Scan the QR code below for a link to a few sunlight lamps in various price ranges.

35 USE BLUE LIGHT GLASSES TO SAVE YOUR SIGHT

This simple tool reduces eye strain, especially if you stare at screens all day. Do you know the signs of screen fatigue?

If you spend more than four hours a day on the computer, you're going to want to protect your peepers from overexposure to what they call "blue light." Eye strain can be a real hamper to working from home if you spend a lot of time staring at screens.

There are a few simple fixes. If you have a smartphone, go to settings, click on the display options, and you should be able to set it to night mode. Don't let the name "night mode" fool you, it's actually great for all times of the day or night.

If you don't have a night mode feature on your computer or device, another good option is to get a pair of blue light glasses. These glasses are specially designed to reduce or eliminate the "blue light" that comes from electronic screens.

Whether you choose to wear them only for a few hours a day, say when you are crunching numbers on a spreadsheet or you keep them plastered to your sexy face all the time as a fashion statement, I'm confident your eyeballs will thank you.

 PRO TIP Keep your blue light glasses in a case on your desk so you'll always know where they are. Also, clean the lenses, you filthy animal.

 BONUS CONTENT Scan the QR code below for a link to my favorite blue light glasses.

36 THE BENEFITS OF AROMATHERAPY

The sense of smell has the power to change your environment.
How can you elevate your workspace with scents?

Music was one of the first ways I experimented with manipulating my mood while working from home. Aromatherapy was one of the more recent. I've always enjoyed the scent of a great candle, but never thought to use one in my home office. That changed when my beloved pup, Emmy, began having accidents in her later years. As my constant office companion, Emmy was always by my side. And even when age started to take its toll, I didn't want that to change.

Infusing your workspace with your favorite scent is a great way to add variety and spice to your day. You can change it up depending on your mood or the time of year. An added benefit is that you can work aromatherapy into your routine and light a candle when you make a big sale or to celebrate a milestone. It can also help to unwind and destress after a long day or at the end of your week. Heck, lighting a candle or incense could become a part of your end-of-day ritual.

If you live in a dwelling where open flames are not allowed, don't fret. Flameless aromatherapy options include melting pots with scented wax, essential oils, or diffusers. There's a reason that fancy stores use the power of scent: it really does affect our mood. Which scent will you experiment with first?

BONUS CONTENT Scan the QR code below for a sampling of my favorite home office scents.

37 PUT A PLANT IN YOUR WORKSPACE

Can a plant save your life? What are the perfect low-maintenance office plants?

Including plants in your home workspace can do wonders for your psyche. They also can improve the air quality, are pretty to look at, and give your office a more personalized, "homey" feel.

The possibilities are endless. My favorite plants are bonsai trees or spider plants, which don't require watering every day. This is perfect in case you take a trip or will be out of the (home) office routinely. You can return to find your plant perfectly intact.

If you like a bit more color, opt for an orchid or a blooming cactus, as both of these need minimal attention and less frequent watering. Whatever you choose, consult your local area plant guide as plant varieties and availability can vary greatly between regions. Ideally, pick something that will grow year-round, maintain roughly the same size over its lifetime, and requires minimal maintenance. When you do need to leave for more than a few days, you can get a watering globe that will release water as the soil dries; these can be sufficient for watering a plant for up to a couple of weeks. If your trip is longer, it's best to have a neighbor stop by and water your plant. You could also gift your plant to a friend or neighbor and pick up a new one when you return from your extended trip.

As for where to buy your plants, you can shop for plants just about anywhere, but at a local nursery you'll get more personalized help and recommendations based on your specific area. But if you're short on time, it doesn't hurt to pick up a houseplant at your local grocery or home supply store.

PRO TIP Some plant varieties do better in artificial light than others. Unless your home office is on the beach or you have a lot of windows that let in natural light, consider this when making your choice.

38 GET A PET. OR A ROCK. OR A PET ROCK.

Having a pet as a coworker adds life and vitality to our work.
Which job title will you give your pet?

Right now we foster Labradors. In fact, my business was named Emmy's Best Pet Products after my dog of thirteen years—she was a white lab, and she was our Chief Executive (Chief Emmy Officer). Emmy passed away in 2019, but having her there in the early days of my company was invaluable. I was never alone with Emmy in the office. The good days were a little bit better with her there, and so were the bad days. When I got off the phone with a miserable client, or I had to attend that meeting that never should have been a meeting—she was there to comfort me with those sympathetic eyes.

It was the best thing ever.

There is plenty of evidence that having a pet can reduce stress and anxiety and generally improve your outlook on life. After all, there's nothing better than hammering away at your to-do list while Fido or Tinkerbell naps in the corner.[2] For many, there is something comforting in having a work-day companion that doesn't talk back or engage in office politics. Another benefit is that a pet can bring us back to reality and get us out of whatever rabbit hole we may have spent the last few hours in. That is, unless your pet happens to be a rabbit! Occasional breaks to take the dog out or refill the cat's water bowl can be a welcomed distraction.

Not all people are pet people. If that's you, then get a pet rock or a houseplant. There are plenty of ways to bring a little life to your workspace, such as real (or fake) aquariums, bonsai trees, pet rocks, or even a small stuffed animal or a tchotchke on your desk. The goal is to have something to keep you company.

---

2. Pamela J. Schreiner, "Emerging Cardiovascular Risk Research: Impact of Pets on Cardiovascular Risk Prevention," *Current Cardiovascular Risk Reports* 10, no. 8 (2016), https://doi.org/10.1007/s12170-016-0489-2.

Just make sure you explain this to your other colleagues so they don't think you've gone crazy when you start referring to your pet rock as "my friend Ralph."

 Pets can be an endearing way to connect with colleagues and clients. Most of them will not only not mind seeing your pet wandering around in the background, but they will also actually enjoy it, and many will feel an even closer connection with you. Get ready to close more sales and snag that raise you've been dreaming of with the help of your adorable furry friend.

 Scan the QR code below for a list of rescues near you where you can adopt a pet and find resources for your work-from-home furry companion.

39 PAY ATTENTION TO YOUR COMFORT

Uncomfortable work conditions are killer. Too comfortable is not good either. How do you find the right balance in workspace comfort?

Like a gymnast on a balance beam or a tight-rope walker high above the ground, it is vital to strike the right balance when it comes to comfort in your home office. This should be a place that you enjoy being and that has everything you need to get your work done in a productive and enjoyable way.

On the other hand, having a place that is too comfortable may make it too easy to doze off for an unwelcome nap or torpedo your productivity to the point that you dread firing up your computer each morning.

I hope that the tips in this section have inspired you to get serious about creating a home workspace that works not only for the tasks you spend time on each day but also for you. Having the right equipment, the right tools, and the right inspiration around you will surely do wonders for your workday and might even have you rethinking your whole relationship with working from home.

BONUS CONTENT Scan the QR code below for a layout of my home office as well as some other pictures of home office setups from well-known work-from-homers.

How does your home office look? Feel? Following the tips in this section, I know you will create a workspace that works for you. While this isn't an overnight process, I encourage you to take a few small steps right away. Get a better chair (even if you steal it from somewhere else in the house). Take a few minutes to organize your workspace. Most importantly, decide right now where your workspace will be, if you haven't already.

With your environment nailed down, you are prepared to take on the world. Or at least those items lingering on your to-do list. Well done!

Only after your mindset and environment are properly prepared should you move on to the next section. Remember, the mindset is our foundation, and the environment is the structure that is built upon that foundation. Now, it's time to get some things done.

PRODUCTIVITY

Productivity is the sexy part of any book about getting more done and being more successful. There are gurus that are self-proclaimed experts on various tricks and strategies related to productivity, and I am not one of them. Remember, I'm not your guru but rather a guide.

The tips in this section are my own tried-and-true, simple principles to getting more done in less time and being happier in the process. Rather than training ourselves to do more, it's important that we also include the "in less time" portion. Simply working more isn't the key to success or happiness.

Instead, freeing up time to devote to other things is the sweet spot. Use the tips in this section to streamline your workday. Some of these things may sound familiar to you—use them as a reminder to make sure you aren't just familiar with their strategy but are actually implementing them in your everyday life. Others may seem foreign—focus on those, and allow your beliefs to be challenged. It is by challenging our beliefs and being open to change that we become better—and that's what we are after: progress, not perfection.

ARE YOU READY? LET'S GO!

40 STAY OFF SOCIAL MEDIA

Social media is designed to distract us. Be honest. How much time per day do you spend on social media?

There's a difference between business-related social media work and farting around posting cat videos on Instagram.

Unless you want to dive head-first down an endless wormhole, stay off social media during working hours. By its very nature, social media is designed to distract us. There are computer algorithms trying every minute of the day to find that next video or ad or post to put in front of our faces to get us to click, subscribe, follow, or engage.

As a general rule, it's good to avoid social media while you're working. Of course, use it for research or important messaging. And by all means, ignore this tip if *the job* you are working on is, say, social media manager.

If you find it hard to completely say no to social media, consider giving yourself a short social media break once or twice a day to check in. But keep it concise and stick to your allotted time, or else . . . wormhole!

Personally, I spend ten minutes or less per day on social media, but I'm weird like that. I am at my best when I spend a very small amount of time per day on Facebook or Instagram. Occasionally, I'll get pulled into a spiral, but I find I'm less productive and less happy when I do that. I know I'm a bit unusual in this respect, but it's good to figure out what your own personal limits are.

41 DON'T (ATTEMPT TO) MULTITASK

It sounds fun and exciting, but multitasking rarely works.
How have you fallen victim to the multitasking myth?

I spent most of my twenties thinking about multitasking. Not about how good I was at it, or how it helped me to become super successful. Rather, I wondered why I was so awful at it! I'd always heard about the best ways to multitask, but I never could get the hang of it. Every time I tried to combine a few things into one task, or dictate an email while sorting through files looking for something, I'd end up miserably failing at one or the other or, usually, both.

Turns out, it wasn't me. Multitasking is simply a myth! Don't let anyone tell you otherwise. Instead, set aside time to complete a task, and put your full focus and attention toward it. Then move on to something else. Avoiding the pitfalls of (attempting to) multitask is not only about speed but also about quality. Think about it. Would you want a surgeon multitasking? How about a pilot or your Uber driver? Your work is every bit as important as theirs, so give it the attention it deserves.

Have a different opinion on multitasking? I'd love to hear it. Shoot me an email at kevin@alwayswearpants.com.

42 THE MIRACLE OF TASK BATCHING

Task batching allows you to get more done in less time.
How can you introduce task batching into your workday?

If multitasking is a myth, task batching might be the silver bullet you didn't know you were missing. **Task batching** is a planning process that groups similar activities together to improve focus and productivity. Most people bounce back and forth between tasks, aimlessly going from one thing to the next depending on what is making the most noise or demanding the most amount of attention in any given moment. And working from home where there are myriad tasks and distractions around you? This isn't going to cut it.

Task batching is a method of taking control of your schedule that allows you to get more done in a day.

Task batching can get really complicated, and there are plenty of experts that know a lot more about the subject than I do. What I can tell you is this: start small. Set aside periods of the day to check email, for instance. When I'm responding to emails, that's all I'm doing. I'm not distracted by social media or phone calls. I'm doing email. And I can get more done on emails in thirty minutes than I would otherwise.

How often do you check your email? Can you condense checking it to once or twice a day? What part of your day is devoted to meetings? Planning? Punching through your to-do list? Set reminders on your calendar and stick to them. Then rinse and repeat. Establish certain periods that you hold meetings. Use your online calendar tool (chapter 63) to make yourself available. Then, establish times for other common, repetitive tasks. Soon you'll train people that you work with to only approach you with certain tasks during these times.

WHEN YOU DO THINGS IS EVEN MORE IMPORTANT THAN HOW YOU DO THEM.

One thing remains the same no matter how long you've been working from home or what your job is, and that thing is this: separating tasks into manageable chunks saves time and helps you to get more done in less time.

 See chapter 64 to really blow your mind as you learn about outsourcing repetitive tasks. Hello to more time and money, and goodbye to working so much.

 Scan the QR code below to access an exclusive interview I conducted with an expert in task batching.

43 SILENCE YOUR PHONE

Putting your phone on silent removes one of the most potent distractions. How many times per day do you glance at your phone?

If you're a salesperson who is closing deals on the phone all day long, then by all means skip this tip. But otherwise, pay attention.

No matter what you tell yourself, your cell phone doesn't make you more productive when working from home. Whether it's checking in on social media, texting your BFF, or binge-watching funny YouTube videos, it's just a distraction. Stop it.

Of course, it isn't reasonable not to look at your phone at all, either. The way to do this is to put your phone on do-not-disturb when you walk into your home workspace each day and check it at predetermined intervals. Similar to task batching, you'll set aside a few minutes in between tasks (maybe when you're on a break), to look at your alerts and notifications. You'll find this minimizes distractions and helps you to focus.

If you're concerned about missing important phone calls or messages from those who depend on you, establish an alternative contact method. You can also set up a VIP list on most smartphones, which allows calls and texts from certain individuals to still come through even when your device is on silent or do-not-disturb.

The point is not to be constantly pulled out of the zone while you're trying to get something done, but also not be so unavailable that people feel they can't ever reach you.

 Use your phone's analytics to see how many times per day you are checking your phone. Then try to reduce that number over a period of a few days or weeks.

44 TAME YOUR TO-DO LIST

If your to-do list looks more like a grocery list, it may be time to rein it in. How long is your to-do list?

Creating a to-do list is part science and part art. I've experimented with many methods over the years and found what works best for me. Here are my best secrets:

- **Paper or electronic:** Some people prefer a digital checklist and may use a task-management tool or a notepad app on their computer or phone. Others prefer the old-fashioned paper checklist. Pick whichever works best for you and your environment, and then stick with it.
- **Start with the fun stuff:** The first few things on your to-do list each day should be items that you enjoy and are relatively easy to punch through quickly. For me, that is journaling and checking sales numbers from the day before.
- **Delegate and outsource:** Once you've punched through some easy, quick tasks, look through your list and spend some time delegating any tasks that are better performed by others. Getting them off your list early will allow others to be working on things while you focus on the tasks that only you can or should do.
- **Find the important stuff:** For me, important tasks are best worked on in the middle portion of my day. These include important meetings and planning sessions. Find your most productive time of day and punch through these tasks then.
- **Clean up your list at the end of the day:** Spend a few minutes at the end of the day reviewing what has been completed. Reprioritize any remaining tasks for the next day so that you begin with a fresh, clean list.

Being intentional about the items on your to-do list and about when you do them will allow you to be more productive. Don't forget to include things like breaks and some fun along the way. Remember: if you don't plan for it, it won't happen.

45 EFFECTIVELY MANAGE PEOPLE FROM HOME

Managing remote employees presents new challenges. How can you keep tabs on remote employees without ruining morale or trust?

When the pandemic of 2020 struck and I began hearing from friends who were working remotely for the first time, most people took it in stride. Managers, however, were freaking out! It's as if their worst fears that people would sit around in their underwear all day, binge-watching Netflix and eating ice cream, would surely come true. Many soon found out that these fears were unfounded.

That doesn't mean that managing a remote workforce doesn't have its challenges—it certainly does. Successful companies, however, have been doing it for years with great results not just for the employees but also for the company's bottom line. Here are a few tips to help you effectively manage employees working from home:

1. **Measure based on results, not time.** So many people, and companies, get this wrong. There are a few professions that make sense to measure productivity based on time. Attorneys and therapists come to mind. For most everyone else, this archaic way of determining and rewarding productivity does no one any favors. Instead, find ways to measure based on results. If your top-performing salesperson closes more deals in three hours a day than most everyone else does in ten, who cares?

2. **Find ways to infuse company culture into the at-home workplace.** Just because there's no breakroom or water cooler doesn't mean there can't be casual Friday or friendly workplace competitions or rituals. Take whatever it is that makes your company unique and find ways to expand that to workers at home. You may even find there are unique opportunities to get creative: Hello, virtual background

competitions for video meetings and pet costume contests for Halloween. When your employees are happy and feel like they are a part of the team, they not only work harder but also stay longer.

3. **Equip your team with everything they need to succeed.** I have always felt that as a manager, my number-one responsibility is to give my team everything they need to do the job well and succeed. When you have employees working remotely, this could mean a computer that is up to the task, or a printer or cell phone. It could also mean the right software and subscriptions to make their work more seamless and less time-consuming. It might even mean a little extra grace when their kids interrupt a meeting or when their dog needs to go out at an inconvenient time.

By embracing the work-from-home culture and finding ways to take full advantage of the many freedoms and flexibilities it provides while finding work-arounds for some of its inherent challenges, you will be rising to the occasion as a manager, and your employees' morale, their productivity, and your bottom line will reap the rewards.

46 TO MEETING OR NOT TO MEETING?

Many workplaces contain far too many meetings, and the home office is no different. How can you determine which meetings are vital, and which are a waste of time?

Often, collaborations that would be better handled by task-management tools and apps end up in a meeting room, virtual or otherwise.

First, answer this simple question: Is this meeting necessary, or is there a better way to accomplish your objective? Meetings are best suited for brainstorming and planning projects, as well as reviewing those projects along the way or at a completion point. Reserve meetings for these important phases and use task-management tools to keep things on track along the way. If a meeting is required, make an effort to ensure that all necessary people are included and that everyone has a clear understanding of the purpose of the meeting as well as a chance to prepare ahead of time.

Next, focus on consistency. We've all been there: maybe it's early morning and we just rolled out of bed, or maybe we're having a bad hair day, and we just don't feel like turning our video on and facing our boss in our current state.

Do we turn the video on? Or not? That is the question.

The answer is different for every meeting and situation.

THE KEY HERE IS TO HAVE CONSISTENCY AMONG EVERYONE WHO IS PARTICIPATING.

There is nothing more frustrating than preparing to be on video only to show up and find that half of the participants have their camera turned off. You might wonder why you took the extra time to do your hair, or put on makeup, while others literally phoned it in. There are many benefits to conducting meetings with video versus just audio. So much of communication is nonverbal. Being able to see the reactions of the people you're speaking with is of real benefit. So, take the time to determine that beforehand and let your attendees know what the expectations are ahead of time to allow everyone to prepare accordingly.

Decide the rules for each meeting and group beforehand and stick to them.

 To have the best video meetings possible, lighting and sound quality are also important. Make sure to reference chapters 29 and 30 to make your meeting the best it can be.

47 USE AN AGENDA FOR MEETINGS

An agenda keeps meetings on track. Think of the last time a meeting went awry. What do you wish you (or someone else) had done differently?

Meetings with no agenda are like the worst episode of *The Office*. It sounds like everyone talking all at once, or no one is talking at all. And there's no laugh track!

A good agenda is made available to participants beforehand so that they can plan and be prepared. It also serves to keep things focused once the meeting begins. Finally, your agenda can serve as a checklist for follow-up after the meeting has ended, with action items and someone assigned to each task, as well as a deadline for the tasks to be completed or revisited.

 PRO TIP If you are hosting a meeting, use an agenda. If you are merely a participant, suggesting an agenda to the organizer or offering to own the task of creating and distributing an agenda can be helpful.

 BONUS CONTENT Scan the QR code below for a sample agenda from one of my ordinary meetings you can use for your next meeting. Feel free to adapt it for your purposes and make it your own.

48 HOW TO PREPARE FOR MEETINGS

Spending time preparing for meetings makes it more likely they are successful. What can you do in advance to improve your meetings?

Have you ever showed up for a meeting and felt like no one knew what was going on? The next hour is just an exercise in futility with everyone staring at the agenda and ticking through the items listed. By the end of it, there's a flood of action items and follow-up . . . which means, you guessed it, another meeting in the near future.

ONE OF THE TRICKS I'VE LEARNED OVER THE YEARS THAT HAS PAID DIVIDENDS FOR ME IS TO SPEND TIME PREPARING FOR MEETINGS.

Preparing a clear agenda and providing it to attendees beforehand offers the opportunity to prepare for the meeting. By spending time thinking about the subject matter, it's possible to actually *get things done* in the meeting, rather than just talking about them.

Here are a few tips:

1. Read through the agenda, and pick out areas where you know your expertise, experience, or opinion will be relevant. Are you prepared?
2. Ask probing questions to gather more information, if needed, before the meeting. This may include reaching out to your coworkers, vendors, or others who you rely on.

3. Anticipate questions that may come up, including alternative views or opinions that may be different than your own. Be prepared to discuss.
4. When a decision can be made during a meeting, do so. Leave only those items that require further research or where there is a lack of consensus and no clear decision maker for follow-up after a meeting or for the next meeting.

Following the above tips and spending time preparing for meetings will make it likely that your job is more productive, and it will save you hours of frustration from useless meetings. It doesn't matter if you are leading a meeting, or if you're the lowest person on the totem pole. When you prepare for meetings, others will take notice, and they're likely to rise to your level, and be prepared next time too.

PRO TIP It's best to be ready for your meeting a few minutes early. This gives you a chance to make certain that your technology is working properly, that you look your best, and that you have everything you will need for this meeting. I also like to think about any distractions that may present themselves during the meeting. Does the dog need to go outside? Do the kids need anything? Is my partner aware that I am about to have a video call so that he doesn't barge in wearing something inappropriate? Is my do-not-disturb sign hung outside the door? Be prepared.

49 TEST YOUR INTERNET SPEED

You are only as productive as your bandwidth. How do you test your internet speed? How fast is fast enough?

We've all been there . . . a painfully slow internet connection.

One time I was just about to host a webinar, the biggest one yet, more than one thousand people signed up, and suddenly I noticed the chat room—it was blowing up with messages from frustrated guests. Internet connection problems. I literally sat there in agony for the first ten minutes of the webinar helplessly watching the spinning rainbow wheel of death as my connection struggled over and over to connect to the webinar software. It was so embarrassing.

Many people knew that their internet speed was more than sufficient for occasional browsing and streaming before they began working from home. Running a home office, however, can be far more taxing and illuminate technical issues, especially if multiple work-from-homers are competing for bandwidth at the same time.

Keep in mind that with video calls, for example, you are sending out just as much data as you are pulling in. So if you have a fast download speed but slow upload speed, problems will persist. Internet speeds vary widely depending on geographic location and service options in various areas. By testing your connection and taking simple steps to improve it, you will know what you are working with.

A simple way to test your internet speed:

- First, make sure it's the internet and not something else. Check all your plugs and hookups.
- Second, go to Google or Bing and type "internet speed test" into the search bar. It will give you a reading on your connection speed. You have two options after this:

1. To increase speed, you can try to plug directly into your router. Or sit closer to the router, or move the router closer to where you're working.
2. Or you can call your service provider and ask them about higher speeds, especially if it's been a while since you set up your internet connection. There are new speeds coming out all the time, but if you don't ask, you'll never know. It's also a good idea to shop around for the best deals every year or two. You may be able to get a faster connection and save a few bucks at the same time.

How much speed do you really need? Mine is set at up to 500 megabytes downloading speed, but I rarely get that, I get 288 downloading usually and 220 uploading. This seems to be my sweet spot, and fortunately, I have never had another situation happen as I had with my webinar. Never again.

 Depending on what you're doing, upload speeds can almost be as important as download speeds, especially for video calls. Most people focus on download speed and not upload speed, but if you're doing Skype calls or Zoom calls, remember, you're pushing data out through that same connection, so when troubleshooting, pay attention to upload speed as well.

 Scan the QR code below to test your speed for free and get tips on improving your internet connection.

50 INVEST IN A GOOD ROUTER

Your router is an essential piece of equipment. Is your router up to the task?

The black box that is connected to the wall, the one you never touch until your internet is going out, and you say, "Where the heck is my router?" That's the router.

Your router may have come from your service provider when you signed up for the internet, or you may have bought it independently. Either way, it can affect the speed and reliability of your Wi-Fi connection.

Nothing is more frustrating than having an internet connection that is unreliable or just plain slow. See chapter 49 for tips on testing and optimizing your internet connection. Just as important as your speed is what happens to that connection once it gets into your home. Investing in a good Wi-Fi router and optimizing its setup will enable you to get more done and worry less about the internet.

A GOOD RULE OF THUMB IS THIS: IF YOUR ROUTER IS OLDER THAN THREE YEARS, IT'S PROBABLY TIME TO REPLACE IT.

Technology is changing every day, and routers can become obsolete and unable to handle the latest technology and fast speeds in a few short years. Don't skimp when it comes to a router. Those with mesh technology can pierce walls and floors and give you a better connection.

Many can now be supplemented with extenders that carry the signal further into areas of your home a greater distance from the main connection.

If you do a lot of video or other data-intensive tasks, consider locating your router in the same room as your home workspace and plugging it in directly. This lets you tap into the fastest speed possible.

BONUS CONTENT

Scan the QR code below for links to my favorite routers.

51 HAVE A GOOD HOME PRINTER

The wrong printer can leave you in a lurch or cost a fortune.
What is the right printer for your situation?

There isn't as much need to print paper in the digital age, but having a printer when you really need one is invaluable. There is nothing more annoying than not having a printer when you need one most.

A reliable printer with the functionality you need is a must-have when working from home. You don't want to waste time messing around with paper jams or ink shortages or have to leave the house every time you need to scan something. Pick a printer with plenty of ink, the ability to print both color and grayscale, and a minimum basic scanning functionality.

Next, make sure you are stocked up with extra ink cartridges and plenty of paper. Place the printer somewhere that is easily accessible but out of the way, such as in the corner of the room or in a closet if your office is a bedroom. A lot of printers are wireless now, which makes it easier to keep it out of sight. I've even seen people hide their printer inside a dresser drawer, but keeping it under your desk so it isn't taking up space will do just fine. It just needs to be accessible when you need it.

For various people, it'll be less important, but we all need to print something from time to time. And for some types of businesses, you'll need a printer constantly (to print shipping labels, for instance). In either case, you should get a printer that is suited for your work.

WHEN CONSIDERING PRINTERS, PAY ATTENTION TO THE COST OF THE INK.

Most printers are subsidized to make their cost lower, because the manufacturers know that they'll make most of their money with ink refills. If you skimp on a cheap printer but pay out the nose each time you buy more ink, you may end up spending more overall than if you bought a slightly more expensive printer to begin with.

Faxing is almost nonexistent these days, but occasionally a need arises to fax something. There are free apps available for both iPhone and Android devices that allow you to scan a document and fax it right from your smartphone. Search for them in your app store.

Scan the QR code below for links to efficient printers that won't break the bank.

52 MONITORS: WHERE THE MAGIC HAPPENS

You're not stuck with the monitor that came with your computer.
How can you adjust your monitor(s) to best serve your work?

In a home office, the magic happens on your monitor. Or monitors, rather.

Unless you're a cartoonist who hasn't moved into the twenty-first century, you do at least some of your work on a computer. And the most important part of that computer is your monitor.

I work exclusively on a laptop, and sometimes it's all I've got, for instance when I'm traveling. When I'm home, ideally, I plug my laptop into a bigger monitor so I have more room. Most people assume that their laptop is all they have to work with. Or if you have a desktop you are stuck with the monitor it came with. It used to be seen as a luxury for computer programmers and film editors, but today you can have a dual monitor setup very easily. You can supplement that with a bigger or better monitor or multiple screens.

THE ONLY GUIDELINE IS THAT YOU SHOULD MAKE SURE THAT YOUR MONITOR MATCHES THE WORK THAT YOU DO.

Perhaps you do basic tasks such as checking email or scheduling social media posts. In that case you can probably make do with whatever monitor you have now or the one that came with your computer. But if you do data entry or work with a lot of spreadsheets, you could probably benefit from a larger monitor or even two monitors. Setting these up properly will allow you to fit more on your screen. If you are dealing with a lot of things at once, like comparing drafts or inputting data from one application to another, dual monitors will make keeping an eye on several different things much easier.

The point is, you're not stuck with whatever monitor you're using currently. Monitors are inexpensive these days, and upgrading to a larger monitor, or multiple monitors, can be done for a fraction of the cost of a new computer. Take the time to think about the work you do and make adjustments to suit your situation.

BONUS CONTENT Scan the QR code below for a list of monitors I like at various price points.

53 HAVE THINGS DELIVERED TO YOU

Order office supplies and have them delivered rather than wasting trips to the store. How can you save time by having supplies delivered?

How much time do you spend each week or month at the store, shopping for supplies? If the answer is any time at all, stop it! Paper, ink, and other office supplies can easily be ordered online and delivered right to your door. In fact, I find that online sources are generally better priced than the big office supply store across town.

Of course, now that you're working from home, it isn't just office supplies that you need. Groceries, clothing, pet supplies, and even household items are all things that we typically spend time shopping for regularly. Think about how much time you would save by having these items delivered to your home. Remember, the goal isn't to become a hermit who never leaves the house. The goal is to save time that you could better put to use for other things.

Wondering what to do with that extra time? Check out chapter 76 for some ideas.

54 DON'T GO TO THE POST OFFICE

Save massive amounts of time by skipping the post office.
How can you handle mail from home?

I don't know about you, but where I live, there are two post offices within a mile of my house. Each time I've ventured into this horribly outdated and often unfriendly abyss, however, it costs me at least an hour of my time. The one or two times per year I find myself at the post office, I'm amazed at how many businesses I see dropping off packages and mail. What are you doing, businesses? I feel like this tip is for you.

Seriously. If you are wasting time going to the post office every day, or every week, you don't have to. You can print postage online for virtually anything you need to send. Whether it's a letter or a package, or whether it's every day or just a few times a month, stop wasting time at the post office.

Set up an account with Stamps.com, get an inexpensive scale, and start printing postage at home. Be nice to your mail carrier. Schedule pickups for free on USPS.com for package pickups, order free supplies, etc. You can do the same with the other major carriers. And if your mail needs are more regular or include different carriers and package types, something like Ship Station will allow you to do it all with a few clicks and even automate things like shipping for e-commerce stores.

Of course, there are exceptions to this. Maybe you have a P.O. box that needs to be checked, and that is part of your job? If so, ignore this tip. For most of us, however, the post office is a place we should rarely, if ever, visit.

BONUS CONTENT Scan the QR code below for a free trial of Stamps.com.

55 THE PROS AND CONS OF VPN

VPNs are a useful security tool, but they can also hinder productivity. How can you navigate your VPN situation?

If you've never heard of a VPN (virtual private network), you probably don't need one. You can skip this tip. If, however, you are familiar with the technology, you should understand how it works and its limitations. If you're overseas, for instance, you can use it to binge watch Netflix from your home country, but usually people use VPNs for security purposes or to hide their location. While useful in many situations, it can also cause your connection to slow, especially if you are using video or trying to stream.

Before working from home was commonplace, many companies mandated the use of VPNs to safeguard data and for privacy. If this is the case for your company, there may be little you can do about it. But if you can, I suggest you get them to reevaluate these policies and only use VPNs when they are necessary.

For projects that require secrecy and security, VPNs are great. But if you're just sending an email to a coworker, it can be an unneeded hassle. In most day-to-day working scenarios, having a VPN isn't necessary, but it's good to know about them!

56 HAVE A BACKUP FOR TECHNOLOGY

If there's one thing I have learned, it is this: technology will fail you. What needs to be part of your tech backup plan?

Your phone will die (or get dropped in the toilet), your internet connection will crash, your files will get corrupted, or your remote control will be eaten by your dog. I don't have to list them all, you've probably got a few technology "fail memories" of your own.

KNOWING THAT TECHNOLOGY WILL SOMETIMES FAIL US, THE BEST THING WE CAN DO IS TO HAVE A PLAN FOR WHAT WE WILL DO WHEN THAT HAPPENS.

You can't always predict, but you can plan.

It can be as simple as making sure you have a phone number for someone you have an important video call with or backing up your files to the cloud. Big companies have a term for this: contingency planning.

Here's some suggestions for contingency plans for when the inevitable happens:

- Get a contact book (the old-fashioned paper kind) or a Rolodex.
- Back up your files to the Cloud.
- Get an external hard drive.
- Alternate communication methods and have more than one way to contact people.
- Keep your old phones so you have a backup for when your phone dies.

While you don't need to get all technical—pardon the pun—you should definitely have a plan.

After having several podcasts that had to be retaped because of power outages, I finally bought a battery-operated power bank (basically a surge protector with a battery built in). If your power goes off, the power bank will keep everything running for a least an hour, so you can finish what you're working on. This doesn't help much if the power outage stretches beyond that, but it is at least enough time to wrap up whatever you were in the middle of.

57 PRACTICE GOOD EMAIL HYGIENE

Just like our own bodies, email hygiene matters. How many unread messages are currently in your inbox?

I have to admit, I am probably not qualified to write even a sentence on this topic. Currently, the email "inbox" number on my phone stands at around 80,000 (and that is down considerably over the past two years). I have always been bad at keeping my inbox clean.

On the opposite side of the spectrum, those that take inbox hygiene to the extreme are called "Zero Inboxers." They have an almost supernatural ability to read, respond to, sort, and file away emails in such a way that by the end of the day, their inbox has zero emails. I am truly in awe of them.

The thought of not having 80,000 emails in my inbox is appealing to me, but I'm just not that person. The best I can do is *organize* my emails, learn how to pick the ones that are important, and ignore the rest. The downfall is that I sometimes miss things, because the only things I seem to be able to delete are spam, advertisements, and things I am quite confident I'll never need to see again. But if you're willing to make the trek toward being a Zero Inboxer, or at least taming the beast that is your inbox, here are a few helpful tips:

1. Unsubscribe to junk/spam emails. If you never open them, why allow them to keep filling up your inbox?
2. Create folders for emails you need to save, and file messages away once you've read and/or responded to them. Many services such as Gmail make this easy with automated rules and filters for emails.
3. Leave only unread emails and emails that need to be actioned in your inbox. This way, a quick glance will tell you what outstanding work you have ahead of you.

4. Utilize technology. Autoresponders, vacation alerts, and email sorting and filing tools can help reduce the manual lifting to keep your email hygiene respectable.

If you spend more than two hours a day reading, responding to, and/or actioning email, consider outsourcing it. Unless that is your core job function (you do that for your boss, etc.), email can be a huge time suck. At one point in my career, I received almost five hundred emails a day, and at least one hundred were important and needed some form of action. I quickly outsourced this task and freed up three to four hours I could spend on other important tasks where I really excelled.

Scan the QR code below to access an exclusive interview I did with a "Zero Inboxer" friend of mine.

58 LIMIT TABS OPEN ON YOUR SCREEN

Too many tabs open at one time can be a productivity killer.
How many tabs are open on your computer right now?

There are two types of people in this world: those who only have a few tabs open on their computer at a time, and people like me, with as many as they possibly can. I'll look at a tab and say, "Well, I might need this later." And before I know it, I've got thirty tabs open. It's ridiculous.

If you are the latter type, just know that having too many tabs open on your computer can really slow it down. Your computer has a way of telling you when you're pushing the limits of its hard drive. For me, I know it when Chrome has completely crashed. Every computer is different, but if you can fry a damn egg on the back of your laptop, chances are you have gone too far.

Try to limit the number of tabs you have open at any given time to just the important ones. The rest you can bookmark by hitting the little "bookmark" star button on the address bar of your browser. That way you can restart your computer if you need to, and quickly reopen the four or five things that need to be open every day. You will find that doing this helps you focus on the most important tasks at hand.

Once you've completed a task, close all the tabs associated with it. To me, this feels good, just like checking something off your to-do list.

If you find it too difficult to muster the will to close tabs, there are apps that will cause tabs to go inactive after a certain amount of time. This leaves the tabs on your browser screen but "pauses" them so they don't take up your hard drive's processing power. This will greatly speed up and improve the performance of your computer.

59 USE A TASK-MANAGEMENT TOOL

Task-management tools save you time and keep you organized.
Which one do you need to track your tasks?

If you rely on email and meetings to keep you and your team's work organized and on track, you may be setting yourself up for failure. Email is great for sending and receiving documents and formal communication. However, the daily tasks and projects that fill up most people's workday are more easily tracked and worked on using a task-management tool, which is usually software that helps you and your team better communicate and work together.

I'VE USED TASK-MANAGEMENT TOOLS TO HELP ME STAY ORGANIZED, REDUCE REPETITIVE TASKS, AND GET MORE DONE FOR YEARS.

I will admit that I was not an "early adopter" to these tools at first, but after seeing the progress I made while using them, I became a believer. By using a task-management tool, I can easily see what items I need to work on or what issues other team members are having that may require some help.

There is a plethora of different options out there. A few of the top ones are Trello, Slack, and Asana. They all have pros and cons. Which one is right for you will depend partly on what you do, who (if anyone) is involved in your work, and how you consume and process information.

Trello is great for teams to manage large tasks with a variety of different timelines. Slack is primarily a communication tool and is a great way for teams to stay organized and communicate without filling up each other's inbox.

My favorite task-management tool is Asana. It combines features of both Trello and Slack, with project management and communication components. The reason it's my go-to is that I find it easier to get excited about work using lists, rather than visually. This is peculiar because I am a very visual learner. For whatever reason, my brain functions better using Asana than Trello or Slack.

Everyone has a different learning style. Test them all out and find out which works best for you.

 I use the suite of tools provided by Google for all word processing and spreadsheets, etc. I haven't opened a Word doc or Excel spreadsheet in years. By utilizing Google's online cloud-based tools, I can access information wherever I am and easily share and collaborate with my team. Best of all, it's free.

60 CHOOSE THE RIGHT COMMUNICATION TOOL

There are many tools for communicating, and some are better than others for certain situations. How do you communicate with others? Is it time to make a change?

Choosing the right form of communication is key to managing your day, instead of letting it run you. What is your most-often used form of communicating while working? Did I hear you say email?

A recent study[3] showed that corporate workers spend an average of five hours per day in email. That's more than half of their day. Reading and responding to email. Are you kidding me? Just stop it.

Email can absolutely kill productivity and is even worse for clarity, speed, and morale. Find other ways: Use task-management tools for ongoing projects instead of mile-long email threads and chat apps such as Voxer, Slack, or other messaging tools for shorter questions or conversations. Get on the phone or use a video-calling app. Even better, have a conversation in person when possible. Then follow up with an email if needed to confirm discussions or finalize transactions.

Save email for the important stuff: official introductions, for example, or communications with important legal or financial dealings. Email, in my opinion, should replace sending someone physical letters in the mail. The problem is, for most of us, it's also replaced phone calls, text messages, Christmas cards, yelling at your coworker across the way, and more.

What is one thing you can do today to choose more appropriate communication methods for your work? Go ahead and start now!

---

3. Abigail Johnson Hess, "Here's How Many Hours American Workers Spend on Email Each Day," *CNBC*, September 22, 2019, https://www.cnbc.com/2019/09/22/heres-how-many-hours-american -workers-spend-on-email-each-day.html.

61 SET UP RECURRING SCHEDULES

By creating recurring schedules, the most important things always get done. What belongs on your schedule every week? Every day?

If you took the time to look at your daily schedule, what would it say about you? Do you make the most efficient use of your time? For most of us, the answer is a big ole no! This is because we usually succumb to the thing that is screaming the loudest, at any given moment. The customer who is upset, the boss who is on edge, the coworker who is known to complain, the report that is due this afternoon . . .

The reality is that, for most of us, there is more than enough time in the day to get everything done, and then some. It's how we manage that time that matters.

Glancing at your schedule, you will likely notice things that recur over and over—sometimes hourly, sometimes daily, and perhaps weekly. Common repetitive tasks include sending emails, inputting data, placing orders, or checking up on projects. Grouping these things into recurring schedules is simply allotting the proper time to complete tasks that occur over and over again, somewhat predictably.

By setting up recurring schedules, you'll make sure that these tasks get done when it is most convenient and conducive to do so. Instead of trying to fit in that report on Friday afternoon, you will have the time set aside for it on Tuesday morning. Rather than returning voicemail at the end of the week, you will have a few minutes reserved for that each midmorning. By reserving time, ahead of time, for recurring tasks, you free the rest of your time up to deal with the tasks that pop up throughout each workday.

62 AUTOMATE WHEN POSSIBLE

Shave an hour or more off of your workday by automating.
What's one process you can automate today?

When is the last time you wrote out a check, put it in an envelope, put a stamp on it, and mailed it in to pay a bill? How about the last time you called a travel agent to plan a business trip? Just a few years ago, these things were common occurrences for many office workers. Today, they're gone, thanks to automation.

New technology makes it possible for us to automate time-consuming tasks. Often, workers are hesitant to embrace automation for fear that it may make them less necessary or make their jobs irrelevant. I challenge you to think of it differently. Instead, I want you to embrace automation as a time-saving tool in order to free up time to focus on other things.

Let's face it, technological advances (including automation) are here to stay. Ignoring them only makes us more susceptible to job change or even job loss. Embracing them lets us keep a seat at the table. When I worked in television, automation was a hot topic. New technology was coming online that made it possible to put a live broadcast on the air with far fewer people—robotic cameras, microphones that came on and off, music that played automatically. Most workers pushed back on automation for fear that it would replace them, and I understand that fear. Rather than thinking about it that way, some chose to embrace automation. After all, there were new challenges and opportunities that came with this new technology. There was now a need for people to program these machines, people to operate them, people to fix them.

One camera operator I worked with used the motivation of automation to go back to school and earn a degree in meteorology. He's now a TV meteorologist who earns several times what he used to. How can you embrace automation to free up time in your day? What can you use that extra time to do to become more marketable, earn more money, and enjoy more of life? Here are a few ideas to get you started:

- Email and communication tools
- Travel planning and booking
- Report generation and analysis
- Budgetary and financial data
- Schedule preparation and changes
- Inventory planning and ordering

There are ways to incorporate automation into many facets of our workdays. The key is to embrace them and see them as a great opportunity rather than something to be afraid and fearful of. Shoot me a text with the first thing you automate: (972) 850-2141.

63 USE AN ONLINE SCHEDULER

Online schedulers give you control over your time. What needs to change to make sure you are in control of your time?

This might sound familiar:

"What day works for you?" "What time?" After eighteen thousand back-and-forths like this, you finally set a date, only to realize they're in a different time zone! And now you have to start all over again.

Trying to coordinate a time to talk to people with similarly busy schedules is very time consuming. At a certain point in your work-from-home life, you may realize that you have more than you can do in one day. That day came for me several years ago when my business really started to take off. I realized I was spending too much time in meetings, setting up meetings, and rescheduling meetings, and I no longer had the luxury of missing a meeting or an important phone call just because I simply forgot to put it in my calendar.

This is when an online scheduling tool saved me.

I strongly suggest using an online scheduling tool to make managing your calendar a breeze. At the time of this writing, a few popular options are ScheduleOnce and Calendly. These miraculous modern marvels allow you to send a link to your calendar to anyone who is requesting your time, and the app does the time zone calculation for you. You also have control over what time is made available, as well as a plethora of options such as sending reminders for upcoming meetings. People can even automatically reschedule if they need to, making it less likely you'll spend ten-plus minutes waiting in a Zoom meeting where you are the only one there. Using a scheduler was a game changer for me. It freed up hours in my week I was spending trying to manage my schedule.

Managing your time is critical regardless of whether you work from home or not. You will find that using a tool like this makes an enormous amount of difference in managing your time well.

If you're going to use one, take the time to set it up properly, and set your availability. For instance, I have mine set so that I can send one link to people if I want a short ten-to-fifteen-minute chat and send a different link to people I want to speak to for an hour or more.

Scan the QR code below for a video walk-through on how I set up my online calendar.

64 OUTSOURCE REPETITIVE TASKS

Outsourcing is a great way to free up your time for more important things. Which tasks can you outsource?

I've been an entrepreneur for many years, but it only took me a few weeks to realize that a good portion of my day involved repetitive tasks. Checking email, responding to email, inputting data, making travel plans—the list could go on and on. And even if you are not an entrepreneur, your day, too, is likely filled with rather mundane, often repeated efforts.

For years, I just accepted this as the way it was. It was only after reading Tim Ferriss's bestselling book, *The 4-Hour Work Week*, did I begin to challenge this status quo. Tim's secret to only working four hours per week is to outsource the time-consuming parts of his "desk job" to overseas workers. Over time, he gains the freedom to travel the world and live the life of luxury, working roughly four hours per week.

While you may not follow exactly in Tim's footsteps (I haven't either), the concept is the same.

IDENTIFY THE TASKS YOU FREQUENTLY SPEND TIME ON AND FIND ANOTHER WAY TO GET THEM DONE.

This could be using automation and tools (think emailing and scheduling), outsourcing to a colleague or someone else within your organization who should be doing what you spend time doing, or outsourcing to another person completely. Whether that's transcription, travel plans, data entry, customer service, project management, email—all of these things can be outsourced inexpensively and free up hours of your time each day.

My favorite hiring platforms are Taskrabbit, Upwork, and FreeUp for any number of tasks.

You may be limited by your company due to rules about confidentiality or proprietary information, so tread lightly when outsourcing if you work for someone else. If that is the case for you, then consider what household tasks you may be able to outsource. Do you still mow your lawn because you "enjoy it"? Those few dollars a week it would take to outsource that task could give you a few hours a month to do something meaningful with the family or to take up a new hobby.

BONUS CONTENT
Scan the QR code below for a list of tasks I outsource.

65 FEED YOUR BRAIN

Our brains need feeding and care, just like our bodies. What are you feeding your brain?

You may be thinking: *Feed your brain . . . what? My brain doesn't eat!*

And you'd be right, if you mean feeding in the traditional sense. But what I'm talking about here is not nourishment in terms of calories and protein but information.

WHETHER CONSCIOUSLY OR SUBCONSCIOUSLY, WE FEED OUR BRAINS A TREMENDOUS AMOUNT OF INFORMATION EACH DAY.

The things we read, watch, listen to—all of that information affects the way we think, feel, and behave. Who we follow on social media can have a big impact on the way we live our lives.

Take a minute or two to think about it. Are the things you feed your brain making you happier, more fulfilled? Do they contribute to a positive outlook on life? Or do they bring you down, make you feel cynical and sad? Do they make you want to curl up in a ball and just forget about everything?

When I consider what I am feeding my brain, I ask myself a few simple questions:

1. Is this part of a problem, or part of a solution?
2. Will this build people up or tear people down?

3. Is this something I would be proud of ten years from now, or will I feel the need to distance myself from the content I am consuming?

I can't stress enough how important being protective of the information you allow into your daily consciousness affects your mood, your mindset, and the work you put out into the world.

The old phrase "junk in, junk out" seems poignant here. Not convinced? Try it out. For the next week, limit your social media interactions and focus on reading and spending time with content that is positive, uplifting, and meaningful. See how you feel and decide for yourself.

 Many social media channels allow you to "unfollow" certain people. This maintains the illusion of a connection or "friendship," but you don't have to see the insane things they post and traffic in daily. Who do you need to unfollow today?

 BONUS CONTENT Scan the QR code below for some of my favorite daily reading material. It's how I feed my brain.

66 STAY HYDRATED

Hydration is not only important for your health but also for productivity. What are the best ways to stay hydrated?

You can't get much done if you're not staying fueled. Equally as important, any nutritionist will tell you, as fueling your body with nutritious food, is staying hydrated. The average adult needs eight 8-ounce cups of water each day to stay adequately hydrated.[4]

This is sometimes called the 8x8 rule.

Keep a full water bottle on your desk. Some people like to add lemon slices, chia seeds, or some other interesting element to their water to encourage proper consumption. There's sparkling water, filtered water, spring water, or plain old tap water.

Not getting enough water can cause tiredness and make you more irritable. It can also have other negative effects on your health such as weight gain, headaches, and even dull skin! Do whatever you need to do to remind yourself to drink more water. Maybe set an alarm on your phone or keep a tally on a notepad on your desk.

Note that the 8x8 rule is expressly for water. H_2O—the good stuff. Downing a six-pack of Dr Pepper during your workday doesn't count. I do love me some Dr Pepper, though!

BONUS CONTENT Scan the QR code below to download an app for your smart phone that will help you track how much H_2O you drink, along with the option to receive reminders to drink up!

---

4. Kris Gunnars, "How Much Water Should You Drink Per Day?" *Healthline*, last updated November 5, 2020, https://www.healthline.com/nutrition/how-much-water-should-you-drink-per-day.

67 CHOOSE SNACKS WISELY

What you snack on and when matters. Be honest. Do you need to swap out some of your snack options?

Have you ever eaten a sweet muffin in the middle of the day and fallen asleep a few hours later?

Avoiding a crash is key to our productivity, and that means eating healthy foods.

YOU'LL NEED FUEL FOR BOTH YOUR BODY AND MIND TO MAKE THE MOST OF WORKING FROM HOME.

All fuel (food) is not created equally, however. Pay special attention to what you eat and when.

Nutritional needs can vary widely depending on a variety of factors and your specific needs, so always consult a physician or dietician for specific advice. The following general dietary tips have proven helpful for me, however.

1. Limit caffeine to the first one or two hours of your workday.
2. Limit carbs and sugar in the morning and at lunch.
3. Add proteins and healthy fats to your diet.
4. Drink lots of water—often when we feel hungry, we're actually thirsty.
5. Keep healthy snacks on hand, but not in the office. Force yourself to leave your work environment and seek out a snack to resist munching throughout the day.

I like to reserve sweet treats for a special reward at the end of the day. If you have a sweet tooth, like me, it's something to look forward to!

BONUS CONTENT

Scan the QR code below to access an interview with an acclaimed nutritionist for additional tips and hacks on improving your work-from-home diet.

68 TAKE FREQUENT BREAKS

Short five-to-fifteen-minute breaks can be a lifesaver. How often do you take breaks? Do you need to add another?

Nothing can make the work-from-home experience feel more like a prison sentence than sitting in the exact same spot all day long, being busy—or worse, pretending to be busy. Taking short frequent breaks throughout the day can give you a refreshing boost of energy, ease the monotony, and help you to refocus.

It doesn't have to be a long break either. You can simply push away from your desk, get up and stretch your legs, or go to the bathroom.

A short five-minute break every hour or two can serve as a way to break up tasks and help you to regroup after calls and meetings. This can be anything to change the scenery; even a walk around the house will do. Or maybe you can knock something off your to-do list that can be done quickly like popping the laundry in the dryer, putting away the dishes, or getting the mail from the mailbox. If you're feeling really ambitious, you might call your mother back.

Getting things done around the house while you're working is one of the best hacks for working from home. However, as we discussed in chapter 25, it's important not to get sidetracked by mixing household and work chores. If you choose to get something done around the house as part of a break, be intentional and specific about what you are doing. And when you're done, head back to the office.

Use breaks as a refresher or to reward yourself after tackling tasks you've been putting off. And don't always reach for the fridge (or that tenth cup of coffee)—taking a break doesn't always have to mean snacking!

Guess what? You're 68 percent done with the book! Time for a break.

69 GO FOR A WALK

Get out of the house and get some fresh air. How can taking a walk make you more productive?

I know an entrepreneur who is religious about his morning walk. If you ask successful people, most of them will have some component of physical activity during the day to help them focus and clear their mind.

It may seem simple, and it is. Going for a walk can do wonders for your work-from-home regimen. Taking a break to stretch your legs and breathe in some fresh air can reset your mind and body and prime you to be more productive. It's also a great stress reducer.

It's remarkable how stationary we can become working from home.

I remember Christmas five years ago, everyone in my family got a Fitbit fitness tracker. Naturally, we started having step competitions, and that was the first time I realized how much we work-from-home people don't move. I would consistently come in last in these competitions. I had to make a real effort to get up and walk every day.

WE'RE SUPPOSED TO GET TEN THOUSAND STEPS PER DAY, BUT IF YOU WORK FROM HOME, IT'S A REAL STRUGGLE GETTING ENOUGH MOVEMENT DURING THE DAY TO HIT THIS GOAL.

For some, a brisk walk around the block before starting work does the trick. For others, taking a few short breaks throughout the day to get the blood flowing is more their pace. Or perhaps you'd like to end your workday with a walk to a nearby park to decompress, review your day, and shut off the work mindset to prepare for your evening.

Whatever time of day you choose is okay, as long as you get your body moving for at least fifteen minutes. It's especially important for us that are homebound, so whatever your style, lace up the sneakers and get moving.

 Scan the QR code below to read about how this tip helped to save this book. Seriously!

70 STRETCH EVERY HOUR

A quick stretch every hour can save your body and productivity.
Why not stand up and stretch right now?

Ever had the doorbell ring and realize you haven't left your desk, or even stood up, in hours? It's easy to become sedentary when working from home. This can lead to back pain, headaches, and fatigue in the short term and even more serious ailments over the long run.

A simple solution is to stand up and stretch, every hour. It may seem silly, but it works. To get in the habit, set an alarm on your phone, each hour during your workday. Within a few days, it will be practically second nature. You don't have to stretch your entire body each time, either. Mix it up by alternating between your legs, lower back, upper back, arms, wrists, and feet. Simple, thirty-second stretch sessions are what we're after here, not full on yoga!

I think you'll find that you get a slight burst of productivity and momentum for a while after you stretch. This may even encourage you to incorporate stretching into a regular part of your workouts and overall lifestyle, and that's not a bad thing, either.

BONUS CONTENT Scan the QR code below for simple, easy stretches you can do in your home office.

71 EXERCISE YOUR BRAIN

Exercising your brain is as important as exercising your body.
What are the most effective brain exercises?

Now that you are taking great care to feed your brain (see chapter 65), it's time to get it into shape. Yes, your brain, just like the rest of your body, needs exercise. And simply doing your job, day in and day out, is not enough. In fact, research shows that doing repetitive tasks can actually weaken your brain.

Instead, we need to give our brain a chance to really get into high gear—to think, process, and make decisions that expand our knowledge. Here are a few of my favorite ways to exercise my brain:

- Puzzles. Whether the old-fashioned jigsaw type or even a crossword puzzle.
- Legos. They're not just for kids. Over the past few months, my partner and I have been completing the Lego Architecture series. And I feel like a kid again.
- Reading—a mix of fiction and nonfiction. My grandfather used to call the television the "idiot box." I always imagined him looking down on me in dismay when he learned that I spent the first ten years of my career working within that box. I love a good movie or TV show. But it doesn't come close to engaging my brain and helping me to learn the way that reading does. I try and alternate between a good nonfiction book about a topic I am interested in and then some good fiction to escape for a bit. Both are great ways to exercise the noggin.

Whatever you do, spend as much time exercising your brain as you do your body. What are your favorite ways to exercise your brain? See chapter 98 about joining our tribe, and then post in the group to let us know.

72 KEEP YOUR HANDS BUSY

Keeping your hands busy, especially during creative tasks, helps you focus. What are some ways to keep your hands busy?

Maybe you have a job where you work with your hands a lot. If so, you may not find as much use out of this tip as the rest of us. If, however, you're like me and your job involves processing information, having conversations, making decisions, etc.—keep your hands busy.

I learned a while back that having something I can do with my hands while I read through emails, review budgets, or even talk on the phone helps me to keep my brain engaged. It's almost as if my hands moving and tinkering are a form of manual power generation that fuels the rest of my body, especially my mind. You may think I'm crazy, but there is actually science to back it up.

STUDIES HAVE SHOWN A CORRELATION BETWEEN WORKING WITH OUR HANDS AND INCREASED MEMORY AND CREATIVITY.

Another study showed that kids who were allowed to fidget with their hands learned more quickly than those who were not.[5] Take that, Ms. McLaughlin (my fifth-grade teacher who never let me fidget)!

Here are a few of my favorite things to use:

- Paperclips
- Pens

---

5. Sumathi Reddy, "The Benefits of Fidgeting for Students with ADHD," *The Wall Street Journal*, June 22, 2015, https://www.wsj.com/articles/the-benefits-of-fidgeting-for-students-with-adhd -1434994365.

- Rubber bands
- Silly Putty
- Play-Doh
- Fidget spinners

A word of caution: be mindful of playing with these things when you are on a video call. Unless your camera is framed tightly around you, fidgeting with these things can make it appear that you are distracted at best, and might be suffering from a stroke at worst. I tend to put these handy hand toys away while I am using video, and instead reserve them for the number-crunching, brainstorming, problem-solving tasks during other portions of my workday.

Do you have a favorite thing to keep your hands busy while you work? Share it with me! Send me a text to (972) 850-2141.

73 THE 80/20 OF WORKING FROM HOME

The 80/20 rule can be applied to nearly everything in work and life. Where can you implement the 80/20 rule in your work-from-home situation?

The "Pareto Principle," also known as the 80/20 rule, simply means that 80 percent of consequences usually come from 20 percent of the causes. This powerful concept can explain why 80 percent of profits come from 20 percent of customers. Conversely, it tells the story of why 80 percent of the burden on a customer service department comes from 20 percent of disgruntled customers.

The uses and usefulness of the 80/20 rule can be found far and wide in many different industries and situations.

So, what is the 80/20 of working from home? Here are a few:

- 80 percent of your day is spent on tasks that affect only 20 percent of your overall productivity.
- 80 percent of your challenges come from 20 percent of tasks/projects/customers.
- 80 percent of your productivity is dictated by 20 percent of your decisions. Think: where is my home office? What desk am I using? Have I planned ahead for this meeting?

Can you think of a few ways the 80/20 rule applies to your work from home? Share them with me: kevin@alwayswearpants.com.

BONUS CONTENT Scan the QR code below to learn more about the 80/20 rule, including an interview I conducted with an expert on the topic.

———

What is your big takeaway on productivity? Whether this was a good refresher for you or it caused you to totally rethink the way that you approach work, you are in the right spot.

As you implement these strategies to get more done, I want you to remember: It's not just about getting more done but also doing so in less time. Our time is the only truly non-renewable resource we have. They're only making so much of it, and each of us has exactly the same amount every minute and each day. That means it's also the most valuable resource we have, and we need to treat it that way.

What can you do today to create more time for yourself? What will you do with it? If that part seems a little uncertain, the next section will help bring it into focus.

PURPOSE

I used to think that money would solve all of my problems. Then I got some money, and the problems were still there. Talk about a conundrum! It was only after I started asking tougher, deeper questions that my life started to have more meaning.

In this section, we're going to dive into purpose. Not quite "what is the purpose of life" deep. Rather, what is the purpose of what we do—and why we are doing it? How does family, money, legacy, happiness, etc. affect the work we do, and vice versa?

I promise you that if you take this stuff seriously, your life will change. Ignore it, and expect more of what you have right now. It's a bit deep, but stay with me. It's worth it.

ARE YOU READY?
LET'S GO!

74 FIND YOUR WHY

Finding your why is all about putting purpose into perspective.
What is your why?

Why do you do what you do? For years, I struggled to answer this question. I chased money, even fame. I dreamed of having a big house, traveling, and never having to worry about bills.

I THOUGHT I WAS ONLY JUST THE RIGHT JOB AWAY, OR ONE BIG BUSINESS DEAL FROM THE LIFE OF MY DREAMS.

A few years ago, I made the short drive across town to visit my ninety-two-year old grandmother, who was in assisted living. I was taking her out to lunch for her birthday, and she wanted ribs. When we arrived at the restaurant, I ordered for her—a whole rack of ribs, with her favorite side, cinnamon apples. She balked, arguing that she'd never be able to finish a whole rack of ribs, but I insisted she could have leftovers to take home for a snack later.

The picture on Fritzi's (as we called her) face when the waiter set a huge plate of ribs down in front of her a few minutes later was priceless. It was then that it hit me. *This* was my why. To have the freedom to spend my time doing the things I loved with the people I loved.

Fritzi passed away about six months after that lunch, and I'm so glad I was able to spend a lot of quality time with her in her final months. Working from home has given me the ability to be present, to show up for the people who matter the most to me. Soccer games and birthday parties, chemotherapy treatments and impromptu "mental health days" with friends, spent playing board games or putting together Lego sets. My brother, a Special Olympics athlete, is my hero. Coaching him and a few friends each May as they competed at the state games in Oklahoma became one of my favorite activities while I was in high school and college, and the ability to work remotely has allowed me to continue that for some twenty years now. That week in mid-May is my favorite time of year.

What's your why? What is the reason you get up in the morning and do what you do? If you've never spent time thinking about this, I encourage you to do so—it will change the way you feel about the work you do.

 Simon Sinek has an incredible book on this topic, titled *Start with Why*. In it, Simon makes the case for how finding your why is so important and gives practical tips on how to zero in on what drives you.

75 PUT YOUR FAMILY FIRST

Whatever family means to you, putting them first clarifies every important decision. What does family mean to you?

The word "family" means different things to different people. I've been lucky to have a supportive family, and I am close with most of them. I have friends who aren't close with their bio-families but have amazing, close connections with those they have chosen to make their family, and this is equally as beautiful and powerful.

For a long time, my family was not my priority. When I was younger, I was 100 percent career driven, and I didn't understand the importance of the connections with the people who mattered the most to me. Sure, I would fly in for holidays and get together when I could, but I didn't make time for them the way that I should have. Over the years, though, especially in times of difficulty and stress, it was my family—both my actual family and the close friends whom I consider to be family—who were there.

When you make your family a priority, work and career are put into the proper perspective. Choices become crystallized and much easier to decipher. Family becomes a sort of forcing function, a lens through which options can be weighed and considered.

Pull out the gratitude list (see chapter 15). Who is on it? Those people are family. Protect them and make them a priority, the priority, even. You'll find that life is much more enjoyable.

If you don't have a good relationship with your family, it's time to get a new one. No, you might not be able to "divorce" your aging parents or legally separate from your crazy self-centered sibling, but you can make a conscious effort to spend time with and get closer to the people who matter the most to you. There's a reason you are grateful for these people being in your life. Show them that gratitude by putting them first.

76 INVEST YOUR COMMUTE TIME

Invest those "commute hours" into something that truly matters to you. What can you do to invest that time to better your life?

One time I hired a rock star television director for a project I was working on but was dismayed when I found out about his commute. He'd be driving almost two hours each direction for four days straight, just to get to and from the television show set.

I was so paranoid, I thought for sure he would quit after the first day. But he didn't. The second day he showed up on time and ready for work. He turned out to be great, but there's no doubt, that was a monster commute. He was spending nearly the same amount of hours driving as he was working.

Some of you, I'm sure, can relate.

According to the U.S. Census Bureau, the average American worker working outside the home spends fifty-two minutes per day commuting back and forth to work.[6] (Maybe that was you until you won the work-from-home lottery.) Over the course of a year, that extra fifty-two minutes per day totals up to a whopping 225 hours! Put another way, it's a total of 5.625 days you previously spent inside your car battling traffic.

What are you going to do with all that time, not to mention the extra gas money you aren't spending? Invest it well.

Start by putting a dent in that backlogged reading list and read some good books, or take an online course, learn some new software or take an art class, or spend your time journaling and tracking progress on a new workout regimen. Or if you're family-oriented, invest that time into your family by having more playdates with your kids,

---

6. "Average One-Way Commuting Time by Metropolitan Areas," *United States Census Bureau,* December 7, 2017, https://www.census.gov/library/visualizations/interactive/travel-time.html.

or taking your spouse on an actual date. Or simply catch up on sleep and take a nap!

Personally, I like to put my extra cash toward three things: real savings and investments, gifts for others and donations to my favorite charities, and then something for myself, like a hobby or a trip I'd like to take. I love to paint, so art supplies are always on my favorites list.

It doesn't have to be monetary, either. You can invest your time into anything you like. Just like your stock portfolio, you should be diversifying your investments. Don't just work more. Working from home can lead to tunnel vision and overworking; instead, you should be investing that time into something that will better yourself and make life more enjoyable.

BONUS CONTENT Scan the QR code below for ideas on how to best invest your commute to improve your health and wellbeing, your relationships, and your life.

77 TRY A NEW HOBBY

Hobbies are a great way to add variety to your life. What are your favorite hobbies?

It's important to have other things to do with your time than just working. A well-balanced life consists of social connections, work, and things that you enjoy doing. When is the last time you tried a new hobby?

Here are a few of my favorite hobbies:

- Putting together puzzles/kits/Legos
- Learning a new skill (non-work related)
- Gardening
- Working on minor home improvement projects that bring me joy

Even if you have a hobby or two that you enjoy, I encourage you to try a few new ones. They say variety is the spice of life—and even lobster starts to taste pretty bland if that's all you eat. Finding a new passion or two is directly connected to finding purpose in our life. After all, passion = purpose.

What hobbies will you try in the next week? Jot them down here:

_____

_____

_____

_____

78 FOSTER ACCOUNTABILITY

Working from home means operating without the built-in accountability of a traditional office. What are some ways you can foster accountability for yourself and your team?

In a typical office environment, accountability is something we usually run away from, not seek out. You might have a cubicle buddy looking over your shoulder, or an HR Gestapo, or a middle manager breathing down your neck. Accountability is the last thing you want.

At home, accountability is easier to avoid. That's why you have to go out of your way to seek it out. Yes, I am telling you to seek out accountability in the form of partners, teammates, coaches, and mentors to keep you on task.

Personally, I seek out accountability in three ways: with myself, with my team, and with a coach or mentor.

First, I am accountable to myself through scheduling and managing my time and tasks well and meeting deadlines. Next, I am accountable to my team and coworkers by letting them know when I am working and being accessible to them to help with projects. Finally, I am accountable for long-term growth in certain areas by working with a coach and mentor.

I try to have a coach for whatever area of my life I'm trying to improve. Whether it's a personal trainer or nutritionist, a personal finance expert, or some other type of expert, working with someone that has more advanced knowledge than you do in an area can give you a leg up and help shorten the time to get from where you are to where you want to go.

 PRO TIP Ask a colleague that works in a similar field, or used to, to coach or mentor you. This can be an informal, non-paid relationship. Talking once or twice a month, sharing advice, and gaining insight is a great way to foster accountability.

79 MONEY, MONEY, MONEY

Money: It's better to have it than not to have it. What role and importance does money play in happiness and success?

When I was a kid, I would sometimes spend afternoons with my grandfather after school. One day, he asked me what I wanted to do when I grew up. I thought about it for a few seconds, and then proclaimed, proudly: "I want to make a lot of money!"

"That's not a job," he said, laughing. "Let me give you some advice, Kev.

"Find something you absolutely love to do. Then find someone who is crazy enough to pay you to do that. If you do that, you'll never work a day in your life."

Of course, life is much more complicated than that rosy, optimistic outlook. That advice changed the way that I looked at life and career, though. I've had jobs I absolutely hated, and many that I loved. I've also had very little money, and more than enough—and I can tell you that I preferred the periods of my life where I loved my job and had more than enough money.

I have also found that there is a correlation between these two things. When I was younger, I chased the dollar signs. I took jobs and chose a career path largely based on what would pay the best. I was always scheming and dealing, thinking that more money would equal happiness. It was only when I began following my grandfather's advice and began pursuing what I loved that the stars aligned.

Take it from me: Start doing what you love, hone your skills, and refine your craft. I think you'll find that you are rewarded with the money and the lifestyle you are seeking. Focus on what you love, and the rest will fall into place.

80 WHAT LOVE HAS TO DO WITH IT

When you put your heart into your work, it's easier to love what you do. Do you love your work?

Do you love your job?

If you didn't immediately think, *Yes! I love my job!*, then I want to plant a seed in your mind: It may be time to start planning for a change.

According to Gettysburg University, the average US worker spends ninety thousand hours working during their lifetime. That is more time than you spend doing almost anything else except for sleeping during your adulthood. That's a long time to spend doing something you don't love.

I'M NOT TELLING YOU TO QUIT YOUR JOB TODAY. I AM TELLING YOU TO START DREAMING AGAIN.

What did you want to do when you were a kid? What do you dream of doing when you have some free time? What would excite you to get out of bed in the morning, especially on Monday morning?

All kinds of head trash may be creeping in right now, as you read these words . . .

"It's too late to start over. I've been doing this too long."

"I won't make as much money if I switch careers now, and I have people who depend on me."

"I went to school for this. It's the only thing I know."

All of these are excuses rather than real obstacles. They may be reasons, but they are not rational trade-offs for your happiness.

Make a plan. It starts with the acknowledgment that you don't love what you do and that you deserve to have passion toward one of the biggest portions of your life. Brainstorm. Write in your journal. Talk to friends and colleagues that you trust. Talk to your spouse or partner. Find an online job skills quiz that can help you zero in on potential careers and jobs if you know you aren't happy with where you are but don't know where to look next.

You may find that you face a temporary setback or pay drop from changing jobs or careers, but I promise you—it's worth it. Find what you love to do, and it will pay dividends before you know it—not just in monetary terms, but in fulfillment, happiness, and quality of life.

Remember what my grandfather told me? I'm telling you, now: Find something you love to do, and find someone crazy enough to pay you to do it.

BONUS CONTENT Scan the QR code below for a free career quiz to help you come up with ideas of things you may love to do.

81 ARE YOU A GOOD OR BAD EMPLOYEE?

I found out I was a horrible employee at age sixteen. Are you a good or bad employee, and what does that mean?

I got my first job at the age of sixteen as a cashier at the local drug store. I enjoyed the job and especially the other people I worked with. What I soon realized, however, is that I was a horrible employee. Not because I took too many breaks or didn't show up on time, but because I thought about things differently than most people.

Most of the other young people I worked with got excited each time we got paid. "I made $300 last paycheck," they would say. "Almost enough for that new stereo for my car!" While I was glad to be earning some money, I saw things differently. I would break down my paycheck, and estimate how much the store brought in during the hours I was working. I would then try and determine what their profit margin was on those gross sales, and by the end of my mathematical exercise, I'd be furious that they were making out like bandits with all the cash while paying me peanuts!

Of course, I've learned a lot about how businesses operate since then, and I don't think they were taking advantage of me quite like I might have thought back then. The lesson I learned, however, was an important one. I was a bad employee. I was hard-wired to become an entrepreneur, a business owner. That doesn't mean that I didn't do a good job at all the various positions I held until a few years ago when I struck out on my own. It does mean that I was always eyeing the exit, dreaming about more.

Not everyone makes a good employee. Conversely, not everyone is cut out to do their own thing, either. When I did finally become an entrepreneur, I became somewhat of an evangelist—trying to convince family members and friends to leave their jobs and start a business too. I was dismayed when they told me I was crazy—or tried to start something only to give it up a few months in. Once, after I shared my frustration with a friend and fellow entrepreneur, he chuckled and said "Kevin, it's a good thing that not everyone is an entrepreneur. If they were, you'd have no one to hire to help make your dream a reality." It's a good thing not everyone is an entrepreneur. If everyone was like me, nothing would get done. Sure, there would be a million ideas flowing freely, but no action would be taken. I am grateful for all of the team members who help us every day. They are not just good—they are *great!*

The point is this: If you find that you're a horrible employee, embrace it. Dig a little deeper and find out what is motivating you. It could be you simply don't mesh well with your company, or that you're burned out in your job. It could also be that, deep down, you're yearning for something more.

Are you a good or bad employee?

82 TAKE A VACATION

It is easy to skip vacations when you work from home. Why are vacations important, especially when you work from home?

Every year it happens. Instead of counting sheep, I'm lying in bed at night counting undone tasks filling up my to-do list. I no longer feel excited or curious when I hear the notification bell on my phone, I feel triggered. Every morning, I wake to dread opening up my inbox and seeing all the unanswered emails . . . I've waited too long to take a vacation, and now I'm burned out.

These days, I've gotten better at scheduling time off, but all too often I used to put my own needs aside for my business. This is actually counterproductive, I've learned. Extended breaks from work are extremely important and have direct implications on our physical and mental health, emotional wellbeing, relationships, and productivity.

One thing I hear a lot from people that work from home is that they take fewer vacations, and this concerns me. It's especially true for entrepreneurs. According to the 2013 Sage Reinvention of Small Business Study, 43 percent of small business owners took less vacation time than they did five years previous.[7] Take a vacation. If you work for a company with an established time-off policy, take the time you are given. If you work for yourself, establish a vacation schedule for yourself and anyone else that works with you.

Sometimes all you can do is a "staycation," but ideally you want to leave your home a few times a year. It is easy to fall into the trap of "thinking" you are taking time off, but if you're "just checking email" or putting in a few hours before the family gets up, you are NOT on vacation. To truly relax your mind, you need to unplug completely.

---

7. "Sage Reinvention of Small Business Survey: Canadian Small Business Owners Report Great Satisfaction Despite a Belief That the Canadian Economy Has Not Improved," *Intrado*, October 21, 2013, http://www.marketwired.com/news-release/2013/10/21/1157285/0/en/Sage-Reinvention -of-Small-Business-Survey-Canadian-Small-Business-Owners-Report-Great-Satisfaction-Despite-a -Belief-That-the-Canadian-Economy-Has-Not-Improved.html.

And if you're shuddering at the thought of the next client meeting or phone call . . . you've waited too long.

Unless you're working for a company with an HR department you should check in with, you'll be on your own for determining your vacation time. Schedule the days you'd like to take time off in late December or early January for the entire year. A mixture of short three-day weekends and longer periods of scheduled time off will give you a nice variety. You can always readjust throughout the year as needs change and your plans evolve, but scheduling it early makes it much more likely you'll actually get to take that trip to the beach or mountains.

Scan the QR code below for a list of ways to make a *staycation* feel more like a *vacation*.

83 KEEP A WORK JOURNAL

Documenting your experience working from home can be a cathartic exercise. Have you ever kept a work journal? Why not start today?

You may be familiar with the benefits of journaling, but have you ever thought about keeping a work journal? I have journaled off and on throughout my life, but I recently discovered the benefits of a work journal.

The process is the same—it's the content that is different. Instead of lumping all your thoughts from your personal and work life into one journal, I find that keeping a separate work journal allows me to expand upon the things that are going on at work and how they affect me. I don't do this every day, but a few times per week, I'll spend a few minutes and jot down what I am working on, how things are going, and any fears or obstacles I am facing.

I think you'll find that you feel a sense of relief when you journal this way—almost as if a weight has been lifted. Of course, journaling in and of itself doesn't really change the facts or situations in our life. It can change us, though. By putting something on paper and having a few moments to focus on and process it, we may come up with new perspectives to the situations we are dealing with, and new solutions to the challenges we face.

Here's a sample work journal I might write today:

December 16, 2020

I'm 80 percent done with the rewrite of the book, and it feels amazing! I finally feel that the pieces are coming together, and I have a renewed sense of optimism and determination to get this done. Should be to the editors next week!

We are close to a new deal with Chewy, just finalizing the last few details. This should be a huge opportunity for us next year—it could increase our business by 50 percent.

I really need to hire an assistant early next month. I am spending way too much time on admin tasks that are taking up the majority of my day. I notice on slow days how much progress I am able to make on bigger projects that really move the needle, but most days there is just too much email, etc., to make that progress. Setting a goal of having the hire complete and onboarded by the end of January.

Planning to take next week off and enjoy the holidays. It's been a tough year for everyone, and I really want to relax and enjoy some downtime.

All for now,
Kevin

Why not try a work journal yourself? In fact, go grab a notebook or a sheet of paper, and make your first entry right now.

 Work journals not only are a great resource for the present but can also be helpful to look back on and gain perspective on where you have been. Looking back six months or a year to see the progress you've made, as well as identifying repeating challenges and pitfalls, can be valuable insight. I end all of my journal entries, both personal and for work, with three letters: "AFN"—All for Now, to encourage myself to continue to be mindful and write another entry soon.

84 HAVE A CONTINUITY LETTER

Having a letter detailing all relevant information related to your job protects your legacy. What should be in your continuity letter?

What the hell is a continuity letter? you're probably thinking.

At the age of twenty-five, I became operations manager for a group of television stations in Texas. As far as I know, I was the youngest person in that position anywhere in the country. I was overwhelmed and had a lot to learn. I made a lot of mistakes but also shared in some great successes along the way. A few years later, I decided to officially retire from the broadcasting industry to pursue other ambitions. I knew I was leaving my post in a better position than I'd inherited it, but there was a lot of work still to be done. I gave three months' notice and began working with the managers under me to prepare for a transition. I was hopeful that the corporate bosses would hire one of my lieutenants to replace me, but they were also flying in people from all over the country for interviews, and they weren't planning to announce a hire until a few weeks after I left.

A few weeks before my departure, as I thought and worried about the continuity of our operations, an idea struck me. I spent the rest of that afternoon preparing a continuity letter, addressed to the next person to hold my job. In it, I left important details about how things operated, key decisions, responsibilities, etc. Over the next few weeks, I supplemented this information with other plans, forecasts, etc. I tried to think of anything that might be important or helpful for whoever would replace me, and included it. Before I left, I let our HR manager, as well as my managing team, know about this continuity letter, and on New Year's Eve, I walked out of the building for the last time.

The thing is, so much is lost every time a position turns over. There is a tremendous amount of knowledge and experience that simply never gets passed on, and new hires are left to re-create the wheel, and re-solve problems, over and over. By thinking about the things that the person who replaces you will need to hit the ground running from day one, you are not only helping that person succeed but also the entire organization. If you care about the legacy of the job you are doing, you owe it to them—and to you—to make sure that their success continues after you leave your job.

I've made a practice of having a continuity letter prepared and ready at each job I've had since then, and many times I have received emails, phone calls, and cards telling me how helpful they have been.

Even if you aren't planning on leaving your job any time soon, a continuity letter also serves as a safeguard in the event that something happens to prevent you from working. Those who are left to stand in your place will benefit from the preparation you put into preparing for that situation, however unlikely it may seem.

85 WHAT IS YOUR LEGACY?

A legacy is a gift you leave the world. Have you thought about the legacy you will leave?

I never thought much about legacy until a few years ago when our beloved thirteen-year-old Labrador, Emmy, the namesake of the pet products company I founded, was battling cancer. During the same time as the fight to give her a few more good months of life, we were battling an almost equally daunting foe—an organization challenging our name through the legal process. All of a sudden, I began to face the reality that Emmy would be leaving us soon, and at the same time, we might lose our company.

It was a reporter covering our plight, asking a simple question, that caused me to think about legacy for the first time. She asked, "What do you hope Emmy's legacy is?" As tears welled up in my eyes, I began to think about the impact that this dog had on my life, as well as our hundreds of thousands of customers. This dog, who had been adopted from the back of a pickup truck in a drugstore in Texas, was now the namesake of a company that bore her name and of products that were sold in the same drugstore chain she was adopted from the parking lot of. *That's a legacy*, I thought.

What will my legacy be, though? I came up empty.

LEGACY IS SIMPLY THE GIFT WE LEAVE THE WORLD. THE WAY WE ARE REMEMBERED. THE IMPACT WE HAVE, LONG AFTER WE ARE GONE.

What will your legacy be?

I encourage you to begin thinking about your legacy. We only have a short amount of time on this Earth. Each minute, we are closer to the end of that time. I don't mean to be glum, but it's the truth. By focusing on the legacy we will leave, I think it's much more likely that we make a lasting impact on the people around us, and the world we leave behind.

Today, I am focused on building up others. On giving back, and on helping to lift up the causes I care about. I know that I have a long way to go, but each day is an opportunity to make more progress toward that goal. And I have a very special Labrador named Emmy to thank for that.

BONUS CONTENT Scan the QR code below for a few of my favorite pictures of me and Emmy.

86 LIFT AS YOU CLIMB

When we elevate the people around us, we make the world a better place. Have you ever benefited from someone who lifted as they climbed? How might you lift up others?

When I think back across my career, I am reminded of the many people who played a role in my success: The teacher who didn't give up on me when I struggled with math. The drama instructor who cast me in leading roles, even when I looked a bit different from most kids. The network executive who hired me, even though I lacked the academic credentials typically required for management positions. I could go on for the rest of this book.

Who has given you a second chance? An opportunity that most might have passed on? Lifting as we climb simply means that as we grow and succeed, we don't forget about everyone else. As you climb the ranks, don't forget to look to the people around you who have helped you to get where you are, and, to the extent you can, bring them along with you.

This could mean recommending a former colleague for a position with a new company you have joined. It could mean heaping praise on someone who was instrumental to the success of a project for which you are given credit for, or mentoring a friend going through a tough time and needing to make a career change. When we lift as we climb, we are literally elevating lives and helping those who have helped us. It will win you friends and more karma than you know what to do with.

Who is one person you can lift up right now?

87   GIVE BACK

When we give back, we benefit not just others but ourselves as well. Can you remember a time when you gave back? How did it feel?

Few things give me more joy today than giving back to the people and causes I care about. For a long time, I chased dollar signs and positions that I thought would make me feel important. I craved control, or the perception of it. And I sought out people that I thought were cool or influential. Then, when I started to achieve some of these goals, I realized just how empty and meaningless they were.

I guess you could say that my way of making up for being so shallow when I was younger is that now I get to give back. I do that through donating time—mentoring others, speaking with strangers who email and ask about starting a business. I do it through donating money when I can, to organizations I feel are doing good in the world, or to people facing unimaginable challenges. And I hope I am doing it, in a small way, by writing this book. The reality is that today I have a life I could never have imagined, and while it's not all due to the ability to work remotely, that has certainly made it much easier.

I hope that by reading this material, your life will be improved in some small way too. If that is the case, I am once again the luckiest person I know. The essence of the words "give back" is *gift*. The amazing thing is that while the person you are being generous to may feel like they've been given the prize, the real gift is the one you receive. I don't know how to explain this logically or with reason. I can only speak from experience. When you leave an unusually large tip for a waiter or waitress you feel deserves a little extra recognition, or donate to someone who is facing life's toughest challenges . . . sure, they get something out of that. But you do too.

— — —

When I began focusing on purpose, my life changed. Work didn't feel like work anymore. Instead, it was a passion. My business prospered. My relationships changed, and I found myself surrounded by people who I enjoyed being with.

If you put into practice the attention to purpose, your life will change too. Whether you are just starting your career or retirement is on the horizon, purpose is important. Without it, you are simply a being doing a thing. That's very boring if you ask me. With purpose, life—and the work you do—has meaning beyond just hours and dollar signs.

What can you do today to be more intentional about purpose? Who will you include in that journey? The next section may give you some ideas of where to start.

COMMUNITY & CONNECTION

I was three months into working from home before I realized it: I was lonely.

I was single, though I had a dog. I had friends, but didn't see them as much because I moved to a house by the lake outside of town. And I had colleagues, but they worked remotely too, and so we interacted virtually. One day, I drove into town and sat, working at a coffee shop for a few hours before it hit me—I missed this! I missed human beings and casual chatter and seeing people smile. I knew I had to do something.

The reality is that working remotely can be truly isolating. It's all the more important, then, that we are intentional about creating community and connection in our lives. That connection is vital, and it's not just to maintain our own sense of well-being and avoid loneliness—it's also the human connection that allows us to fully realize the promise of a purposeful life.

In this section, we will explore some ways to do just that.

ARE YOU READY? LET'S GO!

88 THE 5 PERSON RULE

You are the sum of the five people you spend the most time with. Who makes your list? Is it time to add some names? Remove some?

There is a short rule of thumb that has changed my life in profound ways. It's called the "5 Person Rule." In short, it says that you are the sum of the five people you spend the most time with. Generally, you can remove the people you live with (spouse, children, etc.) from the rule, although if you spend a ton of time with your spouse or work with them, it might be a good idea to include them as one of your five people.

Let's say that is the case, and that leaves you four more people to fill up your list. Who would make yours? When I first heard about this rule in my late twenties, it was a reality check. I was mostly spending time with hangers-on. People I knew on the fringes who weren't the most motivated individuals alive. There were a few old friends, people I'd met through work, etc. Let's just say my list of five people wasn't all that impressive. They weren't bad people, and there was nothing "wrong" with them. But they didn't embody the kind of person I wanted to become, and I could clearly see that was exactly what was happening, as if I was picking up all of their less desirable qualities, just by spending time with them.

What happened next was incredible. I made a conscious decision to start spending time around different people. People I admired, respected. People who lived a life that had something in it I was attracted to. Within a few months, my life began to change in big ways. Opportunities presented themselves. Doors opened. Obstacles became no longer insurmountable. I felt better too. I enjoyed the people I was interacting with on a daily basis, the conversations we were having, and the fun we were having too. When I changed the five people I was spending the most time with, my life changed.

Every now and then, I still check in with myself in this area. It isn't that I have some official list of five people, mind you. But anytime I notice that something is lacking in my life (be it direction, clarity, joy, or passion) or anytime something really starts to go awry in the business (sales way down, people quitting, high stress, difficulty with work relationships), I check in. Who are the five people I'm spending the most time with? Often, I find that a slight tweak or change may be needed.

Who are the five people you spend the most time with? Is it time to make some changes to your list?

PRO TIP Cultivate your list of five people carefully. I always like to have at least one person who is at a similar place I am with work, life, or both. An equal peer you could call them. Next, I like to have one or two people who are where I am trying to get. They've been there and done that, accomplishing some or all of my long-term goals. These tend to be people who are more experienced than I am. Finally, I like to have at least one person in this inner circle who is now where I once was. These tend to be people who are younger or at least less experienced than I am at the current moment. The reason this last section is so important is that it helps me to stay grounded; to remember where I came from. It's so vital not to get "too big for your britches" as my grandmother used to say. That is, to stay humble and kind. Frequent interactions with someone who is going through what you've been through is a great way to stay true to yourself.

89 FIND YOUR TRIBE

A tribe is a close-knit group that has your back. What does your tribe look like?

Ever heard of the word "tribe"?

The first time I'd heard of it in the business sense was when I enrolled in a course with Ryan Daniel Moran about how to sell on Amazon. Everyone in the class was now in Ryan's "tribe." It's nothing more than a "group" but just sounds so much more intriguing.

More than a name, though, Ryan wanted to impart in all of us that we belonged. We were in this together, through the ups and downs. It worked, and I dove in, quickly becoming one of the more engaged pupils in the group. I soon found five other students, "tribe members" who I really clicked with. We started having weekly Zoom meetings to go over the curriculum, encourage each other, and solve problems together. I attribute much of my early success in entrepreneurship to the tribe and the smaller group of peers I surrounded myself with.

Have you ever had a tribe? If not, I strongly suggest finding a group of people that you can belong to, who are working in a similar area as you. It could be a group of insurance agents, teachers, accountants, or managers. Life working remotely can be quite isolating by its very nature. Having a group of people who understand your work life and have your back is critical, and the intangibles of that group being composed of people you like and feel a part of makes it even better and more impactful.

If you don't have a tribe, I want to encourage you to begin today to find one. I don't want you to skip ahead, but I have something that may help a little later in the book. For now, start thinking about the people you most like to be around. Jot them down. What are the commonalities? Why do you enjoy being with them? This will help later. You deserve to have a group you belong to.

Are you ready to find your tribe?

90 JOIN A GROUP

Life is less lonely when you have a group. What are some ways to find groups to connect with?

By now, we've established that working from home can be very lonely. One way to make it less so is to join a group. Groups exist for just about anything you may be interested in, both work related and non-work related. While I want you to find a tribe of people to belong to and have social interactions that are related to your work, it's also important to have a group or two outside of work.

Whatever your passions or interests, there's a group for them. Hiking, mountain biking, crocheting, scrapbooking, dogs, cats, ferrets, creative writing, I could go on and on, and I'm sure you could too.

Groups exist both in person and virtually. I'm always a big fan of in-person groups when possible because that human connection is especially important for those of us who don't get enough of it while working from home. But virtual groups can be a great option when your geographic location or, in my case right now, a global pandemic makes it impossible to gather in person.

What groups interest you? Make a plan today to research a group or two and attend in the next week. Your future self will thank you.

 BONUS CONTENT Scan the QR code below for a list of groups on virtually any topic in your area.

91 HAVE FUN

Who says work can't be fun? In fact, I'd say it had better be fun.

Your work should be fulfilling and rewarding and provide you the opportunity to live the lifestyle you crave. It should also be fun. I meet too many people who see work only as a means to an end, a paycheck. Remember how much time most of us will spend "punching the clock" during our lifetime? Ninety thousand hours is a long time to be miserable.

Most of us aren't lucky enough to have a job that is *inherently* fun—but that doesn't mean we can't take small steps to make it fun.

Set goals for yourself throughout the day, especially for tasks you may dread or not look forward to. Reward yourself when you meet or exceed your goals. Take a break or binge that new podcast you've been wanting to try.

Create a competition with your coworkers around a shared project or joint responsibility. Keep it light and civil—but a little competition can be a great way to spice up the workday and allows you to build a closer connection to those you work with.

Decorate your office with the things that excite you and make you happy. Maybe that's artwork from your favorite artist—or even artwork you create. Use motivational quotes or images to lift your spirits and make the space your own. Remember, this isn't a typical office with its drab paint colors and sterile cubicles. This is *your home office*, so make it feel that way. Finding a few things to include in your workspace and activities to make your workday fun will have you looking forward to your short five- or ten-step commute.

92 MAKE AFTER-WORK PLANS

One of the upsides of working from home is often flexibility.
What are some fun things to plan for after work?

WHEN I AM LOOKING FORWARD TO SOMETHING AFTER WORK, I AM MORE MOTIVATED THROUGHOUT THE DAY, I GET MORE DONE, AND I AM ALSO LESS LIKELY TO WORK TOO LONG.

Here are a few of my favorite after-work activities.

- Go to the park. This is one of my favorites. Fresh air, beautiful scenery, and a little light exercise are a great way to relieve the stress of the day and put life back into perspective. One benefit is this is a great option regardless of whether you are by yourself, with a partner or friend, or maybe walking your dog.
- Work on an art project. A few years ago, I took up painting, and while I am not the best at it, I truly enjoy it. Creating something has a way of soothing the mind and allowing you to reconnect with yourself and the world around you. Have you tried an art project to unwind?
- Volunteer. Go spend an hour at an animal shelter, or delivering meals to seniors, or helping out at a local food bank. I promise you, you'll leave feeling like a million bucks.

What are your favorite things to do after work? Why not plan something for this evening, or for tomorrow?

BONUS CONTENT

Scan the QR code below for a list of charitable organizations in your area that are looking for volunteers. Most of these groups are always in need of a helping hand, so no amount of time is too small.

93 HOST A VIRTUAL HAPPY HOUR

Virtual happy hours are a great way to connect with other people. How can you plan and execute a virtual happy hour?

Hosting a virtual happy hour is not only loads of fun but it can actually bring you closer to friends and work colleagues. And the best part, there's no cleaning up or paying sky-high prices for drinks at the bar. It is super easy to set up a virtual happy hour. Here's how:

1. Decide on a date and time. Create a Facebook event to make organizing easy, or create an email distribution list for the invitees.
2. Create a list of people you'd like to invite. Keep it friendly or mix it up with work colleagues. For a grand time, consider inviting several groups of friends to allow people who may not know each other, but all know you, to attend. Send out the invites via email or through social media.
3. Decide on a platform. I suggest Zoom because it allows everyone to see and hear each other clearly and you can even share a video or play music to make it fun.
4. Test your technology a few minutes before kick-off to make sure everything is good to go.
5. Research a fun party game or create a contest (best dressed, funniest background, etc.) to ensure everyone has a great time. Get creative here—the sky's the limit
6. Share a recipe for a favorite cocktail or a suggested wine that participants might enjoy. If booze isn't your thing, a coffee or tea happy hour can be just as fun.
7. Follow up after the happy hour to thank the attendees and make plans to do it again.

Try hosting a virtual happy hour in the next week or two. I think you'll find that it's the next best thing to meeting up with your friends or colleagues at a local watering hole. And since it's virtual, even those who live far away can attend!

BONUS CONTENT

Scan the QR code below for a picture from a recent virtual happy hour I hosted and a list of fun games for your next get-together.

94 JOIN A COWORKING SPACE

Working from home is not for everyone. Have you ever explored a coworking space?

I have friends who have tried working from home and just can't make it work. Through no fault of their own, it's just not ideal to their type of work, personality, and preferences. That's no reason to rush back to a traditional office, though.

Coworking spaces can be a great middle ground between a traditional office and working from home. There are all different types, but in general they consist of shared areas with places you can pull up a chair and plug in to get some work done, as well as private offices you can rent by the day or month. Many coworking spaces also include break rooms (some can be fancy with beer taps and gourmet snacks) and conference areas you can reserve for when you need more space.

I love working from home, but even I crave a bit of shared energy and collaboration. I am a member of a coworking space and enjoy dropping in a few days a month, sometimes for just a few hours. Being around people, even if I don't work with them, always boosts my mood.

If you're still not convinced that working from home is going to be the best long-term solution for you, check out a coworking space near you.

PRO TIP Coworking spaces can also be a great place to collaborate and meet people for both business and personal purposes. They are often filled with a variety of different working professionals from diverse backgrounds and areas of expertise. Hello, networking! An added benefit is that most memberships include mail service. So you can have your "work mail" sent there, rather than to your home. This is a good idea for both security and privacy reasons, and it is also more professional.

95 FIND A MENTOR

Mentors are guides that help with work and life. How do you find one? What facet of your life could benefit from mentorship?

One of the tricks I've used to fast-track growth and success over the years is mentorship. Put simply: If you want to do something, find someone who has already done it, and learn from them. There are gurus such as Warren Buffet and Tony Robbins who have built empires using this methodology. It's worked for me. When I wanted to break into e-commerce, I found some people who were already doing it successfully. I learned from them. When I wanted to learn real estate, I found a mentor. When I wanted to write a book (this one), yep, you guessed it, I found a mentor.

A mentor can be anyone. Sometimes they are a friend or colleague, sometimes they are still practicing whatever it is you want to do, and sometimes they may have retired or moved on. A mentor can also be a casual, unpaid role, or they may charge a fee for their time and support. When you want to learn something new, never feel like you have to start from scratch. Likely, there is someone out there who has "been there, done that"—why not learn from them?

The benefits of having a mentor are plentiful, but here are the top two:

1. You learn from their mistakes and (hopefully) avoid making the same ones.
2. You can emulate their success, putting you on the fast track to achieving whatever goal you have.

When looking for a mentor, I keep a few things in mind:

1. Look for someone with the heart of a teacher. No one likes putting up with difficult, negative, condescending people. So

look for someone who will approach the relationship with a firm but supportive attitude.

2. Ask yourself, "What can I give that will make this situation worthwhile to them?" Sometimes that is paying them. Sometimes it's trading a good or service that is of value to them. Make sure this is a win-win for both of you.

3. Look for the winners. I don't intend to seem brash, but you want to find a mentor who has had success in their area of focus. Don't hire a mentor to teach you how to open a restaurant if their last three ventures failed. This is not to say that all mentors won't have some failures in their life or career. They will, and they should. In fact, those failures represent important lessons that you can employ on your own journey. However, they need to have a proven track record that you can rely on. Find the winners.

4. Take action. This is the big one! All the best advice in the world will do you no good if you don't put it into practice. Make it a habit to listen to the advice of your mentor, engage in meaningful discussion, and then take action.

Have you ever had a mentor? If not, consider finding one and reaching out to them. I think you'll find them worth their weight in gold.

96 BE A MENTOR

If you ask me, the only thing better than having a mentor is being one. How can you be an effective mentor?

If you think your life will be improved by seeking out and learning from a mentor, you're right. Perhaps the only thing better than having a mentor is being one.

You have knowledge and experience that is extremely valuable. When you share it openly and willingly with someone else, expecting nothing in return, you'll get so much more than you can imagine. Ever done something nice for someone? Open a door, pick up something they dropped, or helped someone out when you see them struggling? It feels good, doesn't it?

That feeling times one hundred is how I would describe the feeling of having a mentee and working with them over a period of time. Each time you give advice or counsel and then see them take that advice and succeed, it's one of the greatest feelings in the world, even better than when you may have succeeded with that same thing in your own career.

If you decide to become a mentor, and I hope you do, here are a few things that have helped me:

- Be upfront about your availability and any limits to your time and ability to help. You don't want to take on more than you can handle, and it's better to establish those expectations up front.
- Have the heart of a teacher. To be an effective mentor, your job is not to fix problems or to do the work. Your job is to share your experience, make suggestions, and, most importantly, to help your mentee to learn.
- Be firm, but uplifting. Your mentee is bound to make mistakes, we all do. Your job is not always to prevent the fall, but to

soften the blow through encouragement and advice. Have high expectations of your mentee but know when to be firm and when to be encouraging.

Are you interested in being a mentor? If so, be open to the possibility that an opportunity may present itself for you to invest time into someone to help them to grow. I'd love to hear about your first mentee experience. Email me: kevin@alwayswearpants.com.

97 A WORD FOR PROSPECTIVE ENTREPRENEURS

Entrepreneurs are my passion. Are you an entrepreneur? Do you want to be?

If you are already an entrepreneur, I'm giving you a big virtual high-five right now. You rock! And if you've ever thought about being your own boss, I want to invest in you. Email me and let me know. I'd love to share some advice with you.

Why am I so passionate about entrepreneurs? Because they change the world every day. Seriously, entrepreneurs are the connectors of our society, and they change the world with every problem they solve, innovation they create, and idea they promote and drive.

An example I like to use to illustrate my feelings on this topic is this: Imagine there is a deadly, worldwide pandemic ravaging virtually every country and group of people on Earth. People are forced to stay home as everything grinds to a halt. Entrepreneurs step up and provide vital resources and tools for people to be able to work from home, have food delivered, and easily donate money to those that need it. Other entrepreneurs begin making masks. Governments quickly identify the pathogen and begin working on a cure. The problem is, their resources are limited, and they only have so much capacity to test possible vaccines. Entrepreneurs step in and save the day with the ability to move quickly, scale up or down with ease, and invest private dollars into the effort. A vaccine is successfully created, but there is a lack of infrastructure and expertise to scale its release. Entrepreneurs step in here too—designing innovative packaging and using already-existing shipping networks to speedily disperse the vaccine around the world.

The bottom line is that entrepreneurs fill a void between governments and agencies, nonprofits and educational institutions. Entrepreneurs sometimes get a bad rap for being greedy or only focused on profits. The reality couldn't be further from the truth. Entrepreneurs put their own livelihoods on the line each day for the chance to offer something to society with no promise of it being successful. A steady paycheck every two weeks is not something an entrepreneur can rely on. Instead, they wake up and have to make something happen.

For those reasons and others, entrepreneurship is not for everyone, and that is okay. There are many ways that people make big impacts in the world, and entrepreneurship is only one. I do hope that if entrepreneurship is something you are interested in at all, you'll pursue it. I truly believe you can change the world.

— — —

Even the most introverted people crave connection. Wherever you fall on the scale of personality, your life is meant to be shared with others. Spend some time and get honest about your needs.

What type of community do you want to be a part of? What type of connection do you crave? What needs will be met when you do so? I hope you will use the tips in this section to make them a reality.

ACTION

You've got the tools, now it's time to put them into practice. You can certainly do that on your own, but I find it much more fun to do it with others. To that end, I have a few suggestions on how you can take some first, initial steps.

98 JOIN OUR TRIBE

If this book connected with you, I invite you to join our tribe.
Are you ready to find your people?

Have you found your tribe yet? If not, I want to invite you to join me in our tribe. There is a good group of us that hang out online to share stories, laugh at funny pictures, and support one another.

I'd be honored if you would join us. I want to warn you: we don't take ourselves too seriously, and we believe in having a good time. We strive to be supportive and are welcoming to all people who are willing to join us in our mission to enjoy working from home and use this amazing opportunity to better our lives and the lives of others.

If you're willing to join us, go to alwayswearpants.com and click on *Tribe*.

99 TEXT ME

Seriously, text me. I'll text you back. Have your phone handy?

I find that one of the most intimate forms of communication is through text. So, text me. I like to share funny things and sometimes tips or things I am working on.

So, open up your phone and shoot me a text: (972) 850-2141.

Speak to you soon!

100 SHARE THIS BOOK WITH ONE PERSON

Sharing is caring. Pass along this copy, or better yet, buy one for a friend.

I want to thank you for buying this book. It means the world to me, and I hope that you've gotten one-tenth of the enjoyment out of reading it as I have had writing it. More importantly, I hope that it has been helpful to you. Perhaps in a small way, like adding a plant to your workspace or establishing healthier boundaries with those you live with. Or perhaps in a big way, like the decision to find a job that you enjoy, or to find a new passion to pursue.

If this book has been meaningful to you, I have one last favor to ask: share it. Buy a copy for a friend or neighbor, colleague, or coworker you think might benefit from it. If you manage a team that works remotely, consider buying one for each member of your team. If you can't buy a copy, share this one. I don't care a thing about the royalties from the book—what I hope that you'll share is the message. Right now, there are people everywhere who need to hear about the joys and pitfalls of working from home. They need to hear what we've heard and learned. They need a tribe.

If you choose to help me to spread that message, thank you.

Whether you take the above suggestions on action or not, the most important action is the kind you take toward implementing the tips in this book to better your life and the lives of those around you.

Remember that this is a process, not a single act. Evolving and growing takes time and requires consistent effort—more than just reading a book. The key is to start, and you've already done that, so my encouragement for you now is to keep going.

CONCLUSION

Always wear pants. It seemed like a logical place to start. When a global pandemic hit in the spring of 2020, hundreds of millions of people all over the globe found themselves working from home for the first time. Wanting to do something to help, I began jotting down ideas of tips that would help newcomers to this lifestyle that I had already become accustomed to. I asked friends and colleagues for their suggestions too.

I browsed articles and pored over social media posts for ideas and inspiration. The truly remarkable thing is that, in my effort to help others, I learned a lot myself. Things that I knew but had failed to actually practice. Other things that I once practiced but had been neglecting. And a ton of things I'd never heard of or imagined. It turns out, this really is a journey and not a destination.

I want to thank you for being a part of this journey and for allowing me to be a part of yours in some small way. As I write this, there are signs of hope regarding the pandemic. In the past few months, many countries have vaccinated the majority of their population, and life is starting to feel more normal. For many people, part of their new normal is working remotely. It's not going anywhere, with some of the world's largest and most influential companies already announcing it as a permanent option for their employees.

All the more reason to get serious about doing it right. Starting with getting our minds right and building a solid foundation. Then building upon that with the right environment, which allows us to get more done in less time with productivity. Not just productivity for productivity's sake, though—it's got to have a purpose. And that purpose is best when it's shared with a community through connection.

ARE YOU READY? LET'S GO!

Oh, and one more thing. Take your damn pants off if you want to. You've earned it.

ACKNOWLEDGMENTS

I owe an immense amount of credit to the individuals listed below. To Mr. Hankins, for always believing I had something to offer the world. To Austin, thank you for being the moon to my sun. To my parents, for all of your support. To Azul, for believing I had a book in me, and patiently helping it come to fruition. To John Rossman, for your friendship and enthusiastic support. To Rich, for always making me look better than I do. To Karen, for your steadfast friendship. To Mackley, thank you, old friend. To Mom, who made me read when I didn't want to. To Dad, for always encouraging me to do big things. To the entire team at Mandala Tree Press: Azul, Steve, Amanda, Kim, Emily, Kam, Christine, Justin, Kaitlin, and to my team: Rich, Rachel, Karen, Austin, Ammy—you are the unsung heroes, working behind the scenes, without whom this book would just be an idea. To Anne, for your brilliant direction and advice. To Shannon, for getting me started on the right foot. To those who have been with me since Day 1, and to all that have joined in the journey, thank you!

ABOUT THE AUTHOR

Kevin Rizer is an entrepreneur, speaker, and thought leader whose content has reached millions of people worldwide. In 2015, Kevin founded and hosted the popular *Private Label Movement*, interviewing some of the biggest names and brightest minds in the e-commerce world. He has appeared on stages throughout the world sharing with audiences on topics of e-commerce and finding the passion and purpose in work. Today, he is the founder and CEO of a pet products company sold throughout the US, Europe, Australia, and Japan.

Kevin is best known for sharing openly about the ups and downs of entrepreneurship, and his down-to-earth, relatable personality have won over fans among thought leaders and audiences alike. Having worked from home for more than a decade, Kevin is passionate about helping others discover the art of working remotely and being happier in the process. Kevin lives in Dallas, Texas, with his partner, Austin, and their labrador retriever, Mika. When he's not working, Kevin enjoys being outdoors, binge-watching true crime dramas, and supporting causes important to him in the animal welfare, entrepreneurial, and neurodiverse communities.

I would appreciate your feedback on what chapters helped you most and what you would like to see in future books.

If you enjoyed this book and found it helpful, please leave a **REVIEW ON AMAZON.**

Visit us at **ALWAYSWEARPANTS.COM** where you can sign up for email updates.

Connect with me directly by email:
KEVIN@ALWAYSWEARPANTS.COM

THANK YOU!